TRUE CHAMPIONS KNOW THE TEAM
IS STONGER THAN THE INDIVIDUAL

TEAMWORK

CHAD BONHAM, GENERAL EDITOR

FELLOWSHIP OF
CHRISTIAN ATHLETES

THE HEART AND SOUL IN SPORTS

Regal

From Gospel Light
Ventura, California, U.S.A.

Published by Regal
From Gospel Light
Ventura, California, U.S.A.
www.regalbooks.com
Printed in the U.S.A.

All Scripture quotations, unless otherwise indicated, are taken from the
Holman Christian Standard Bible®, Copyright © 1999, 2000, 2002, 2003 by
Holman Bible Publishers. Used by permission.

Other versions used are
KJV—King James Version. Authorized King James Version.
NIV—Scripture taken from the *Holy Bible, New International Version*®.
Copyright © 1973, 1978, 1984 by International Bible Society. Used by permission of Zondervan Publishing House. All rights reserved.
NKJV—Scripture taken from the *New King James Version*. Copyright © 1979, 1980, 1982 by Thomas Nelson, Inc. Used by permission. All rights reserved.

© 2009 Fellowship of Christian Athletes.
All rights reserved.

Library of Congress Cataloging-in-Publication Data
Teamwork / Fellowship of Christian Athletes.
p. cm.
ISBN 978-0-8307-4630-9 (trade paper)
1. Sports—Religious aspects—Christianity. 2. Teamwork (Sports)
I. Fellowship of Christian Athletes.
GV706.42.T43 2009
796.01—dc22
2008033770

1 2 3 4 5 6 7 8 9 10 / 15 14 13 12 11 10 09 08

Rights for publishing this book outside the U.S.A. or in non-English
languages are administered by Gospel Light Worldwide, an international
not-for-profit ministry. For additional information, please visit www.glww.org,
email info@glww.org, or write to Gospel Light Worldwide,
1957 Eastman Avenue, Ventura, CA 93003, U.S.A.

CONTENTS

THE FOUR CORE 5

INTRODUCTION: THE ME MONSTER 9

1. COMMON ENEMIES (OF TEAMWORK) 12
   Tony Dungy
   Winning Super Bowl Coach of the Indianapolis Colts

2. STRENGTH IN NUMBERS 24
   Shaun Alexander
   NFL Running Back

3. THE FIVE Cs 36
   Les Steckel
   President and CEO of Fellowship of Christian Athletes

4. KNOW (AND ACCEPT) YOUR ROLE 48
   Cat Whitehill
   U.S. Women's Soccer Team Defender
   and Olympic Gold Medalist

5. TRUST OR CONSEQUENCES 60
   Andy Pettitte
   Major League Baseball Pitcher

6. EYES ON THE PRIZE 72
   Luke Ridnour
   NBA Guard

7. CHECKS AND BALANCES 84
   Curtis Brown
   NHL Defender

8. TWO-WAY STREET 98
   Sam Hornish Jr.
   NASCAR Driver and Former IRL Champion

9. ALL FOR ONE 110
   Tamika Catchings
   WNBA Forward and Olympic Gold Medalist

10. THE TIES THAT BIND 122
   Mark Knowles
   Former Men's Doubles Tennis Champion of the
   U.S. Open, French Open and Australian Open

11. SOARING WITH EAGLES 134
   Steve Fitzhugh
   Former NFL Safety and National Spokesperson
   for One Way 2 Play—Drug Free

12. FIRM FOUNDATIONS 148
   John Wooden
   Former UCLA Head Men's Basketball Coach

THANKS 156

IMPACTING THE WORLD FOR CHRIST THROUGH SPORTS 158

FCA COMPETITOR'S CREED 159

FCA COACH'S MANDATE 160

THE FOUR CORE

Dan Britton
Senior Vice President of Ministries, Fellowship of Christian Athletes

The NCAA Final Four tournament is an exciting sporting event. Even if you are not a person who likes basketball, it is awesome to watch March Madness as it narrows down 64 teams into 4 core teams. This makes me think about Fellowship of Christian Athlete's "Four Core"— not four core teams, but four core values.

Core values are simply the way you live and conduct yourself. They are your attitudes, beliefs and convictions. Values should be what you are, not what you want to become. The goal is to embody your values every step of the way.

Are your values just words, or do you actually live them out? Can others identify the values in your life without your telling them? Your values need to be a driving force that shapes the way you do life! Talk is cheap, but values are valuable.

When everything is stripped away, what is left? For FCA, it is integrity, serving, teamwork and excellence. These Four Core are so powerful to me that I have made them my own personal values. So, I have to ask you, what are your values? What guides you? Let me share with you FCA's Four Core, which are even better than the Final Four!

Integrity

To have integrity means that you are committed to Christlike wholeness, both privately and publicly. Basically, it means to live without gaps. Proverbs 11:3 says that integrity should guide you, but that a double life will destroy you. You need to be transparent, authentic, honest and trustworthy. You should be the same in all situations and not become someone different when the competition of the game begins. Integrity means to act the same when no one is looking. It is not about being perfect, but, as a coach or athlete, you need to be the real deal.

Serving

In John 13:12-15, Jesus gives us the perfect example of serving when He washes the disciples' feet. He then commands the disciples to go and do unto others what He has done to them. How many of your teammates' feet have you washed? Maybe not literally, but spiritually, do you have an attitude of serving just as if you were washing their feet in the locker room? You need to seek out the needs of others and be passionate about pursuing people who are needy. And, the last time I checked, everyone is needy.

Teamwork

Teamwork means to work together with others and express unity in Christ in all of your relationships. In Philippians 2:1-5, Paul encourages each of us to be one, united together in spirit and purpose. We all need to be on one team—not just the team we play on, but on God's Team! We need to equip, encourage and empower one another. Do you celebrate and hurt together as teammates? You need to be arm-in-arm with others, locking up together to accomplish God's work. There should be no Lone Rangers.

Excellence

To pursue excellence means to honor and glorify God in everything you do. In Colossians 3:23-24, Paul writes, "whatever you do, work at it with all your heart, as working for the Lord, not for men." The "whatever" part is hard, because it means that everything you do must be done for God, not others. You need to pursue excellence in practice, in games, in schoolwork and in lifting weights. God deserves your best, not your leftovers.

It is tip-off time for the game of life. How will you be known?

> *Whatever happens, conduct yourselves in a manner*
> *worthy of the gospel of Christ.*
> PHILIPPIANS 1:27, *NIV*

Lord Jesus, my prayer is to live and compete with integrity, serving, teamwork and excellence. It is a high standard, but I know that with Your power and strength, it can happen. I want all my relationships to be known for things that are of You. Search my heart and reveal to me my values. I lay at the foot of the cross the values that do not honor You, and I ask for Your forgiveness. The values that bring You glory, I lay them at the foot of the cross for Your anointing.

THE ME MONSTER

Everyone should look out not [only] for his own interests, but also for the interests of others. Make your own attitude that of Christ Jesus.

PHILIPPIANS 2:4-5

One of my all-time favorite stand-up comedians has a routine about what he calls the "Me Monster"—the kind of person who is completely lost in his or her own world, consumed with his or her own desires, and who does all the talking for everyone else. Me Monsters are everywhere, especially in the athletic world. They lurk in every sport, on every team, in every organization. They are completely self-absorbed and focused on themselves instead of their team. In fact, they are enemies of true teamwork.

I'll never forget my first encounter with a teammate who was a Me Monster. He was a member of my college lacrosse team. I'd played with self-centered guys who didn't care about the team, but I'd never before met a full-blown Me Monster.

Now, when I talk about Me Monsters, I don't mean the kind of ball hogs we all know who never pass to their teammates. I'm not even talking about the ones who brag about their accomplishments and think that they are incredible athletes. I'm talking about the players who, after a brutal loss, are excited because they scored their goals. That's how my teammate felt. His excitement about how well he played and what he did on the field as an individual was evident, regardless of the team's performance. And if we won a big game and he didn't score or play well, he would be visibly upset in the locker room. He flat-out did not care about the team and was not the least bit concerned about teamwork. He was happy only when he played well as an individual.

This guy had incredible skills as a lacrosse player. Yet because of his selfish pursuits, he was not a great player. He wasn't even a good player. He was a dangerous player who broke down teamwork and the trust and loyalty within the team.

God taught me a lot through this teammate. Through his example, I realized how much of the same selfish nature was in me, and the Lord showed me that I needed less of me in me and more of Jesus in me. As humans, we speak more than nine million words a year. Half of them, statistics show, are possessive: "I," "me," "my" and "mine." I don't know about you, but I'm sick of talking and thinking about myself. And maybe, just maybe, others feel the same way, especially when it comes to teamwork.

In order to maintain healthy team dynamics, we all have to be aware of our own Me Monster tendency. In life, "we" is more powerful than "me," especially when it comes to teamwork. My college lacrosse teammate lived by the me-rather-than-we philosophy, which could just as well be the me-rather-than-He [Jesus] concept. And unfortunately, sports are usually all about the "me." As a coach, an athlete or a leader, it is hard to die to self every day. But that is the only way God's best can be achieved. Think of how great it would be to have a team of "we"-focused athletes instead of those who are "me" focused.

Living out the concept of teamwork is to say, "We did it!" God can best use us when we sacrifice our own interests. He calls us to pick up our cross daily and follow Him. The popular acronym T.E.A.M. isn't found in Scripture, but you can't help but realize that it certainly applies: Together Everyone Achieves More.

11

HOW TO USE THIS BOOK

Teamwork takes an in-depth look at this core value and comes at it from 12 different angles as lived out by 12 different people. Their insights shed new light on this value and give us a model to follow.

You can read *Teamwork* individually or as part of a group. As part of a personal devotion time, you can gain insight as you read through each story and ponder on the "Training Time" questions at the end. Mentors can also use this book in a discipleship relationship, using the "Training Time" questions to step up to the next level. And small groups (huddles) can study the core value as a group to be prepared to sharpen each other with questions.

1

Common Enemies
(of Teamwork)

Tony Dungy
Winning Super Bowl Coach of the Indianapolis Colts

We must pursue what promotes peace and what builds up one another.
ROMANS 14:19

Gettin' good players is easy. Gettin' 'em to play together is the hard part.
CASEY STENGEL

When a lanky quarterback turned defensive back from the University of Minnesota named Tony Dungy arrived in Pittsburgh for the Steelers training camp, no one would have blamed him for being a little overwhelmed. After all, that team featured 10 future Pro Football Hall of Fame inductees: Terry Bradshaw, Franco Harris, Lynn Swann, John Stallworth, Mike Webster, "Mean" Joe Greene, Jack Lambert, Jack Ham, Mel Blount and Head Coach Chuck Noll provided the nucleus of a team that would claim four Super Bowl titles.

Dungy was a part of the 1978 team that defeated the Dallas Cowboys in Super Bowl XIII. He led the team in interceptions that season and a year earlier became the only player in NFL history (since the AFL-NFL merger) to throw an interception (while filling in for injured quarterbacks Terry Bradshaw and Mike Kruczek) and intercept a pass in the same game.

While most would assume it was the star power that turned the Steelers organization into a dynasty, Dungy says it was the attitude of selfless cooperation that made the team virtually unbeatable. He knew that to be true because he already understood—from previous experience— what true teamwork looked like.

"I was fortunate," Dungy says. "I played a lot of team sports when I was young. I think sports do teach you that. The coaches that I had early on really did stress winning. They stressed skill development and those types of things, but they always taught that you win together. That's one of the great things about Fellowship of Christian Athletes and about athletics, especially the team sports. Everyone working together is imperative if you're going to have a good team."

While many people tend to state the obvious when it comes to teamwork—first emphasizing working together toward a common goal—Dungy believes the true essence of the word must emerge from each team member's intentional acts of selflessness.

"Teamwork doesn't mean you don't have individual goals," he clarifies. "It means you're willing to put your individual goals behind the goals of the team. If you can do that, you'll be a great teammate, and you'll have great teamwork. That's what we're always looking for on our football team—people who can put their individual goals and hopes behind those of the team, which are winning and being the best team that we can be."

As the head coach of the Indianapolis Colts, Dungy used those biblically inspired concepts to help his team claim the Super Bowl XLI trophy. He readily cites 1 Corinthians 12:4-6, where the apostle Paul—in an effort to diffuse dissension among the Early Church in Corinth—reminds the members that "there are different gifts, but the same Spirit. There are different ministries, but the same Lord. And there are different activities, but the same God is active in everyone and everything."

"It's really all over the Bible," Dungy says. "Not everyone's going to have the same gifts or abilities. Paul talks about what it would be like if we were all the same thing. Everything is needed. All parts of the body are needed for the body to function well. Christ talked a lot to His disciples about not wanting the preeminent position but being willing to serve. It's all for God's glory, and we're all working together. There seems to be a constant emphasis on how everyone has a part."

Dungy's philosophy is also driven by biblical principles presented in such key Scriptures as Romans 2:11, which tells us that "there is no favoritism with God." Everyone has great value in God's eyes and has been called to be a part of His kingdom.

"The big thing that I see when I read the Bible is that Jesus always pointed out that everybody was important," Dungy says. "And that's what you are trying to sell to your team—that everybody has a role. No matter how small you think it is, even if you're not necessarily the star, you are important. . . . And that's what good teams have. It's not a matter of having the most talented guys but of having the most cohesion, the most ability to work together."

But in order to work together, the team must first have a coherent understanding of the overall vision. The question, *What are we playing for?* must be answered; and the subsequent answer must be accepted and wholeheartedly embraced by every single individual.

"If we have a common goal—just like Christ and His team had the common goal of spreading the gospel—and if we work together, we can do great things, and no one can stop us," Dungy says. "But if we are fragmented and we've got different agendas and ideas and we're not working together, no matter how much talent we have, we are not going to be successful."

Dungy says there are many issues that have the potential to divide a team, "especially in professional sports."

"Number one is the paycheck," he says. "If the football team is your source of income, then you're going to want to do everything to maximize that. A lot of times that goes back to individual goals—publicity, desiring to be in that star position, ego, pride. A lot of what we associate with worldly ideas really gets in the way of teamwork.

"Another enemy of teamwork is individualism. As a team, the whole has to be greater than the sum of every individual part. The only way to do that is to work together, and by working together you can get more done, and you have fewer distractions and less negatives. It's the same way whether it's a church body, a family body or anything that you're trying to get done. You can go a lot farther pulling together than you can with individual people pulling separately."

These things collectively chip away at team unity until the proverbial cracks in the armor begin to show. Sometimes the chipping is subtle and is disguised as legitimate individual concerns. In more than 30 years of experience within the NFL, Dungy can attest to the increasing difficulty of keeping teams together and, more importantly, keeping teams unified over a long period of time.

"We all want to do well," Dungy says. "We all want to provide for our families; and players often feel that 'the better I do, the better I can provide for my family.' That's true, and you don't want to take that part away; but you don't want to look at that so much that we lose the team concept. And you've got other things like the media and outside forces that tell players they should be playing more, they should be getting the ball more or 'You could be helping your team if they used you more.' We have to worry about that to a great extent.

"We also have agents now that say the same thing," adds Dungy. "They want what's best for their client, and that's their job. But their job isn't to see the team win; it's to see their client do well. So we've got to embrace that and still focus everybody in the right direction. Those are big challenges. It's not easy getting everybody on the same page, working together, but the teams that do it successfully are the teams that win."

Every attack on team unity can inevitably be traced back to the basic element of pride. One of the *American Heritage Dictionary's* definitions of pride is "arrogant or disdainful conduct or treatment." Other definitions are "an excessively high opinion of oneself" and "conceit."

Dungy says that pride rears its ugly head in two specific ways. The first is when teammates fall prey to the lie that their job isn't as important as the job belonging to the so-called stars on the team. "Sometimes you get a situation in which some players say, 'Well, I'm not a starter or I'm not a key component, so maybe my job is not important,'" Dungy explains. "You have to make them feel that it really is. You really do need them. Even if their job is small, the player needs to do it exceptionally well in order for the team to be successful."

But 2 Corinthians 10:12 warns us not to "classify or compare ourselves with some who commend themselves. But in measuring themselves by themselves and comparing themselves to themselves, they lack understanding." This line of thinking keeps many people from reaching their fullest potential. It also leads to mediocrity, which can result in feelings of insecurity and even depression.

The opposite is true for those who fall under the more traditional definition of pride—those who are bent toward arrogant and conceited mindsets. Habakkuk 2:4, however, tells us that one whose "ego is inflated . . . is without integrity."

"Some athletes always feel that everything depends on them, because they are in that star position," Dungy says. "You need to let them know there's not as much pressure as they might feel. It's telling them, 'You've just got to do your job. Yes, it's a big job, but we have other guys who also have to contribute. You aren't the only one out there.'"

Sometimes pride can be easily detected, but many times it remains hidden within the heart. Because of that fact, Dungy believes that there is an element of spiritual warfare that takes place as it relates to teamwork.

"Satan can use things that are good, like 'I want to do my job well,'" he says. "But if I take that to extremes, that can get in the way. There are all kinds of things that can be good in and of themselves, but Satan can direct that away from the team's goals. That's what you're always on the lookout for, those subtle little things that can get in the way of team unity."

All of these factors also come into play when teamwork is transposed to a much greater level of significance—that is, within the larger Body of Christ. In the same way that teams fail to reach their goals due to distractions brought on by pride and individualism, so too is the Church often diverted from its goal of reaching the world with the gospel message of hope and salvation through a relationship with Jesus.

That's why it's so important to live by Romans 14:19, a passage in which the apostle Paul instructs us to "pursue what promotes peace and what builds up one another."

"Just watching children, we understand that our human nature is not bent toward teamwork," Dungy says. "It has to be nurtured. You have to develop it. You have to constantly work on it. It takes practice. It's the same thing in the church setting. You have to really emphasize it and be on the lookout for the little fine things between the lines that get in the way.

"It's human nature to put yourself first," he continues. "But Romans tells us not to think like the world thinks but to transform your thinking. That's really what you have to constantly try to do."

Dungy's reference to Romans 12:2 may not always be linked to the principle of teamwork, but the truth of the passage is nonetheless an effective tool in establishing unity and warding off its common enemies such as pride, confusion and a lack of vision: "Do not be conformed to this age, but be transformed by the renewing of your mind, so that you may discern what is the good, pleasing, and perfect will of God."

In order to stay in a Christ-centered frame of mind, Dungy understands that he must maintain a constant attitude of prayer or "pray continually," as we are admonished in 1 Thessalonians 5:17 (*NIV*).

Dungy takes his cue from Jesus' prayer found in John 17:21-23, which provides believers a template of how to pray for unity within a team or any group of people: "May they all be one, as You, Father, are in Me and I am in You. May they also be one in Us, so the world may believe You sent Me. I have given them the glory You have given Me. May they be one as We are one. I am in them and You are in Me. May they be made completely one, so the world may know You have sent Me and have loved them as You have loved Me."

"I pray a lot for our team," Dungy says. "I pray in the evenings for direction. I pray for individual guys. I pray for that common bond and that sense of unity. I pray that we'll bring the right guys in the mix, the guys that we need both spiritually and athletically. And I really pray a lot that we keep our focus. That's probably the biggest thing that I pray for, because I feel like if we do that, we're going to be successful."

Dungy's players have undoubtedly felt the power of his prayers. Colts' linebacker Tyjuan Hagler is certainly no exception and says his coach's unique leadership style fosters an atmosphere of peace and cooperation.

"I hear a lot about how other teams always argue, and there's always a lot of stuff going on in the locker room," Hagler says. "People are unhappy with the coaches, or they're unhappy with each other. But everyone on this team reacts to each other as one. Everyone sticks together no matter what the situation. If there's a problem that we need to correct, we talk about it. We don't point fingers like other teams do. We don't blame the coaches. We put it on ourselves to get better as a team."

Hagler's description makes Dungy's work sound easy, but the seasoned head coach knows all too well the difficulties that accompany the task at hand.

"It is the biggest challenge," Dungy says. "Fortunately we've had a good team here for a few years and so you're a close-knit group; and you're in the playoffs, and everybody understands how fun it is when you do win, and that snowballs. But many times, the biggest thing is getting everyone to focus on the ultimate goal of winning and not the little smaller goals that are individually oriented."

And to do that, Dungy clings to the Word of God for instruction, guidance and encouragement. One passage that sums up his belief in teamwork and how it can be achieved is found in Romans 15:5-6, which states, "Now may the God of endurance and encouragement grant you agreement with one another, according to Christ Jesus, so that you may glorify the God and Father of our Lord Jesus Christ with a united mind and voice." While winning is certainly important to Dungy, that Scripture ultimately reminds him of the true purpose behind teamwork.

"The things that I talk to my players about, the qualities we're going to need to be a good team on the football field," Dungy says, "those are the same qualities we're going to need if we're going to be an effective team for spreading the gospel."

TRAINING TIME

1. When Tony Dungy talks about playing for the Pittsburgh Steelers (see the "In His Own Words" section), he explains that the team's success had more to do with teamwork than talent. Can you think of some teams that had great talent but failed to succeed?

2. What are some individual goals that could hinder a team's goals? Can you describe a time when you were asked to sacrifice personal goals for the greater good of the team? How did that impact the end result?

3. Read Romans 2:11. Have you ever been on a team in which the coach had favorites? If so, how did that make you and the other players feel? How did it affect the team's ability to work together? How does Romans 2:11 cut against the grain of the world's tendency to pick favorites?

4. What are some enemies of teamwork that you have encountered? How did those negative elements affect team chemistry and the team's overall success? Read Romans 14:19. In what ways can you promote team unity and peace and build your teammates up?

5. Read Romans 15:5-6. Which of God's characteristics does the apostle Paul say can bring forth unity? What are some of God's other attributes that we depend on while striving for unity and peace?

"When I came to the Pittsburgh Steelers, I was a rookie, and I came in during the heyday when they were in the process of winning four Super Bowls in six years. You think of all the star players and the Hall of Fame guys and you think, *Well, that's why they're so good.* But it really wasn't. When I got there, I saw how it operated. It was the practices. It was everybody working together. It was the offensive guys helping the defensive guys. It was the close-knit nature of the team that made us hard to beat much more so than just the individual star players. That's the lesson that I took from it, and that's stayed with me my whole coaching career. I think it's still possible to achieve that today. The good teams have that. Even though you have star players, they understand that it's not 11 individuals who are going to go out there and have things run smoothly enough to win. It's going to be how you practice, how you work together, how you encourage each other, how you help each other to become a team and to become a unit. You have to constantly talk about team goals and where you want to go as a team and how we can be effective. You have to look out for the warning signs and try to nip those in the bud when you see that individualism creep in."

—Tony Dungy

2

STRENGTH IN NUMBERS

Shaun Alexander
NFL Running Back

And if somebody overpowers one person, two can resist him. A cord of three strands is not easily broken.

ECCLESIASTES 4:12

In union there is strength.

AESOP

Shaun Alexander has always been a winner. If you ask him the secret of his success, he will probably list more than just one—including the vital component of exemplary teamwork.

Teamwork has been a part of Alexander's competitive life as long as he's been donning pads and strapping on a helmet. It fueled his success at Boone County High School in Florence, Kentucky, and vetted his Southeastern Conference (SEC) championship run at Alabama in 1999. The same holds true for the Seattle Seahawks' 2005 National Football Conference title that led to a berth in Super Bowl XL.

But if you ask Alexander about some of his most memorable teamwork moments, he's just as likely to refer back to a much simpler—but nonetheless impressionable—time.

"You might get a bunch of friends together to play hide-and-seek," Alexander says. "You might be playing with 10 kids, but you've got three friends that you're going to work with and make sure that everybody gets back to the base. I remember one of my friends was about to get caught and the other friend jumped out of his hiding spot, knowing he was fast enough to get away. He created that distraction, and it allowed all three of us to get back safe."

When asked about his earliest model of teamwork, however, Alexander's answer is quite predictable—especially for anyone who has read the early chapters of his 2006 autobiography, *Touchdown Alexander: My Story of Faith, Football and Pursuing the Dream*.

"My mom is a servant," he reveals. "I used to see her give so much to other family members, and I knew she didn't have the money to give, but she would still give it. But she was doing it because our family had an 'all for one, one for all' attitude. That's what teamwork is all about. It's about everybody achieving the goal at hand."

Alexander eventually discovered that his mother was living out a principle that can be traced back to the Bible. In particular, he often references Ecclesiastes 4:12, which says, "And if somebody overpowers one person, two can resist him. A cord of three strands is not easily broken."

"When you get three people pulling in the same direction with the same goal, then that's teamwork," Alexander explains.

It's the age-old truth that asserts there is inherent strength in numbers. Teamwork is so much more effective and efficient when a band of brothers joins forces in order to achieve a uniform purpose.

The concept immediately sends Alexander back in time when he first served at Fellowship of Christian Athletes camps during his college days at Alabama. That experience was the beginning of a spiritual paradigm shift.

"When I started doing FCA camps, I got to meet some other brothers in Christ who were just like me," Alexander says. "Some were successful college athletes just like me, and I saw them chasing after Jesus and growing in God but still discipling and mentoring other people. We were all in it together. I got stronger by just having them around me."

Alexander was so greatly impacted by his early FCA encounters that he has continued his involvement with the organization and, in fact, utilizes its invaluable resources to work with young people today. He has found that this generation of athletes often benefits from the same spiritual community-building structure that changed his life.

"I send about 50 kids to an FCA camp every year," Alexander says "I think about the Huddle Leaders, which were kind of the first generation of kids that I mentored and discipled. When they all get there, they get to meet other kids who I mentored from all across the country, and they get to meet people just like them from other states. That is the strongest thing for them; and when they get together, it's powerful, because they have that same focus and drive and discipline. Now they have numbers."

Ever since his old FCA camp days, Alexander has not only extolled but also employed the concept of strength in numbers. He has surrounded himself with trustworthy friends who will keep him on the straight and narrow path and engage in brutal honesty when necessary.

"There is more than one person who mentors me and speaks into my life," Alexander says. "If I have an issue, I can have five mentors who call up, and they all give me different perspectives. It takes many advisers to win the war. That doesn't mean you should ask 100 people for advice. But there's some godly counsel that you can have around you to pour into your life, and it will keep your steps straight. That's what happens with strength in numbers."

Alexander's philosophy is a paraphrase of Proverbs 24:5-6, where King Solomon uses a military analogy to wisely exhort people to seek sound guidance for every part of our lives: "A wise warrior is better than a strong one, and a man of knowledge than one of strength; for you should wage war with sound guidance—victory comes with many counselors."

And although the word "accountability" may not be found in most biblical texts, the concept is certainly woven throughout its pages.

27

"If some issues are popping up, we can all come together in agreement and pull each other out of a bad situation," Alexander says. "That's a powerful thing. A lot of times, Christian men don't get enough men around them. They might just have one. So if the problem is drinking, the one struggling might ask the other to help him out, and the next thing you know, the one that's struggling has pulled the other one down. But if there are three brothers around, they're all going to pull you up."

Accountability has other benefits as well and easily transfers to the athletic world. For Alexander, this has been especially important as a running back who is often the target of hard hits, nasty tackles and undetectable rule bending that regularly takes place at the end of a play.

"In football, the pile is probably the most dangerous thing," he explains. "But there was a time with the Seahawks when I'd get tackled, and I'd be on the ground by myself. It's because my five linemen never allowed people to pile on me. So I'd get tackled, and they'd be pulling guys off of me immediately. They weren't going to let people beat me up under the pile. They had my back."

It was that type of camaraderie that the Seahawks exhibited during the team's 2005 run to the Super Bowl, where the team lost to the Pittsburgh Steelers. That year, Seattle won the NFC's West Division behind Alexander's MVP performance, which included an NFL-best 1,880 rushing yards and an NFL-record 28 touchdowns (the latter since broken by LaDainian Tomlinson).

Even going into that 2005 season, Alexander had a feeling that something special was going to happen.

"People just humbled themselves," he recalls. "They got around each other and had authentic conversations and learned about each other's families and kids. When you start getting around each other like that, you can't help but become a true team and actually win, and that's what was happening."

According to Alexander, much of the team's strong sense of community came from its even stronger Christian influence. For those eight seasons, from 2000 to 2007, the franchise experienced numerous highs and lows but as a whole remained faithful to a calling of godly excellence.

"Our team was full of Bible-believing, strong Christian men," Alexander says. "Anytime you've got a team like that, it is easy to grab your brother and just pray—pray for you, pray for your family, pray for your teammates, pray for the guys who aren't saved on the team. But then also, you can start holding each other accountable to love authentically. I think that's what drew our team closer together.

"We called things what they were but all in love," he adds. "We didn't expect unsaved people to act like Christians. We expected Christians to act like Christians. I think that is one of the things that made it easy to play for the Seahawks—brothers who were standing strong. We were going to hold you accountable to be strong. And then the ones who weren't [Christians], we were going to love them even harder, because we wanted them to have the goods that we had."

Alexander doesn't reserve the right to hold Christian brothers accountable and confront them if needed to just in the locker room. He carries it over to his personal life, where that close-knit band of friends he relies so heavily on gets involved in the big issues and the minute details— even when that means taking risks and getting caught up in the fray.

"There was a friend of mine who had done something stupid," Alexander says. "It was definitely ungodly. It kind of shook the whole family up, and we weren't sure what we should do. We all loved this person, so three friends and I decided to go meet with him. We all went out to dinner and I told him, 'It doesn't matter what you do. I'm going to keep you with us. We're going to keep you in the truth. We're going to keep you in the family. We're going to find you and pull you out of the darkness.' That's the definition of having somebody's back."

Alexander's experience is reminiscent of one of the many parables that Jesus told His disciples. Alexander was prompted to share one particular story (found in Matthew 18:10-14) after they questioned the amount of time He was spending with the children: "See that you don't look down on one of these little ones, because I tell you that in heaven their angels continually view the face of My Father in heaven. [For the Son of Man has come to save the lost.] What do you think? If a man has 100 sheep, and one of them goes astray, won't he leave the 99 on the hillside and go and search for the stray? And if he finds it, I assure you: He rejoices over that sheep more than over the 99 that did not go astray. In the same way, it is not the will of your Father in heaven that one of these little ones perish."

Alexander's strong belief in this principle is precisely why he has made the conscious decision to get actively involved in the lives of young people. He initially did so through the Shaun Alexander Family Foundation, which assisted families who lacked for basic needs, granted scholarships and held toy drives and food drives. Now known simply as the "Shaun Alexander Foundation," the organization partners with national organizations to fund programs that promote athletics, education, character and leadership for youth 8 to 24 years old. Alexander has also continued to personally pay the FCA camp tuition for several young athletes.

Alexander is also developing a new program called Club 37 that will speak specifically to the issue of mentoring young men who lack a solid adult male presence in their life—something he has already been personally doing since his playing days at the University of Alabama and plans to continue long after his NFL career is over.

At the opposite end of the spectrum from Alexander's teamwork model is a dangerous mentality that many people are tempted to embrace—flying solo, or going it alone. Even within the team concept, sometimes athletes succumb to this line of thinking by refusing to conform to team rules, resisting instruction from the coaches or simply isolating themselves from the other athletes. Alexander says going it alone is a sure-fire unity killer on a team but is equally deadly when it comes to spiritual matters.

"Some people are like, 'You know what? I'm just going to love Jesus. I'm going to read the Bible. I'm going to pray. I'm going to study,'" he says. "God's first commandment is to love Him; but His second one is just as important, and that's to love others—love people. So there's no way that you can do it all by yourself."

When people resist the benefits of teamwork, Alexander suggests they are falling into a trap tailor-made by Satan. So often, followers of Christ think that avoiding the "big" sins is the most important element of the Christian life. But according to Alexander, it's often the little things—those things not always associated with sin, such as pride and selfishness—that cause us to stray from the path that leads us along God's perfect will for our lives.

"When you go it alone, you really can't see when you're one degree off," Alexander says. "That's the power of a marriage. You hopefully have two people who have the same passion for Jesus, but because they're so different, they can always tell when things are a little off. It's the same thing when you take a group of guys who are keeping each other accountable. They're going to recognize when someone isn't quite right."

So what about those who feel as if they're all alone in the fight and don't think they have anyone to team up with in this spiritual battle? While Alexander under-stands those individuals' plight, he also believes that it's ultimately not a valid excuse.

"Most of the time, you're never really alone," he says. "You just haven't found those people. And a lot of times people want to find another God-loving person, but they want them to look or act like them. There's a danger in that, because that's usually pride. That's when the need for friends ends up being for selfish reasons, while God is saying, 'I'd rather you have a need for friends to do my work, not so you can get friends and then push Me into the corner and never talk to Me anymore.' "

At the end of the day, however, Alexander says there's only one thing that really matters when it comes to hav-ing strength in numbers. Anyone who is truly walking with God in this journey through life is going to have all the support he or she needs to successfully win the race. There's logic-defying strength in understanding the na-ture of His sovereign power.

"The One who has set the plan for your life into mo-tion is the One who said 'Let there be light' and there was light," Alexander says. "It doesn't really matter if you have a majority or not or if the numbers make sense or not. He's the same One that said, 'Shaun, you go mentor young men who are going to change the world.' I don't need to have numbers anymore. I don't have to be able to explain any-thing. As long as I know what God says, I can hang my hat on that."

33

TRAINING TIME

1. Shaun Alexander talks about how playing hide-and-seek with his friends was one of his earliest memories of teamwork. What are some unique, non-sports-related examples of teamwork in which you have participated? What other ideas come to mind?

2. Read Ecclesiastes 4:12. What does the phrase "strength in numbers" mean to you? Can you describe a time when relying on this concept made you and a team or group more successful?

3. Have you ever tried to go it alone when chasing after your goals? If so, what challenges or frustrations did you face along the way? Read Proverbs 24:5-6. What does Solomon suggest as an effective way to approach such scenarios in your life?

4. Read Matthew 18:10-14. Jesus told this parable as a way of explaining the importance of children in the kingdom of God. What biblical teamwork principles can you also pull from the story?

5. What are some dangers that teammates could protect each other from? Spiritually speaking, what are some dangers (seen or unseen) that we face as believers? How can you apply the concept of "strength in numbers" as a way to protect yourself and your fellow brothers and sisters in Christ?

"The more players you can get on the same page, the better chance you have of becoming a champion. You take Alabama my senior year. There were only 19 seniors on the whole team. We only started five seniors. That's just five guys leading a team that won the SEC Championship and went to the Orange Bowl. People always wondered how we did that. We had everybody on our team believe that somebody had to play a perfect game to beat us. That's what happens when everybody gets together and believes the same thought. On a true team, everybody's needed. Your role is needed too. God designed you to do a specific role, but when you try to do someone else's role, that's when selfishness comes in or a lack of self-esteem comes in or a feeling of being unneeded or unwanted comes in. If the kicker says, 'I want to be the quarterback,' then he's damaged everything, because he doesn't realize his value and he's damaged the value of the quarterback. Selfishness always comes from you forgetting who you are. But when you know who you are, you know that you're a part of this great team. You could be the heart of the team. You could be the brains of a team. You could be the arms of the team or the legs of a team. Your part is needed. There isn't one part of the body that isn't important."

—Shaun Alexander

3

THE FIVE CS

Les Steckel
President and CEO of Fellowship of Christian Athletes

If you love me, you will obey what I command.
JOHN 14:15, *NIV*

*The task of the leader is to get his people from where they
are to where they have not been.*
HENRY KISSINGER

Over a 32-year stretch of time, Les Steckel has coached championship football at the high school, college and professional levels. As different as each of those experiences has been, there's one philosophy he has always shared with his players. "I used to tell my players, 'Let me take you where you can't take yourself,'" Steckel says. "That requires a willingness to cooperate and be committed."

Steckel could make such a bold statement because chances were he *had* already been where most of his players wanted to go. Born in Whitehall, Pennsylvania, in 1946, the Fellowship of Christian Athletes president and CEO began a lifelong journey of unique experiences at the University of Kansas, where he graduated in 1968 with a triple degree in human relations, political science and social work.

After college, he enlisted in the Marines and served in Vietnam as an infantry officer. After returning from active duty, he joined the United States Marine Corps Reserves in 1972 and stayed involved with the military until retiring with the rank of Colonel in 1999. Steckel often talks about the esprit de corps that he learned while serving with the Marines—a French saying that the *American Heritage Dictionary* defines as "a common spirit of comradeship, enthusiasm, and devotion to a cause among the members of a group."

On the professional level, Steckel found great enjoyment in his career as a football coach—first within the NCAA Division I ranks at Colorado (1973 to 1976) and Navy (1977) before moving up to the NFL in 1978 as an assistant with the San Francisco 49ers. That job led to a string of opportunities, including stops in Minnesota (1979-1984), where he served as head coach in his last year there, and New England (1985-1988), where he coached the Patriots' offense in Super Bowl XX.

After a brief return to college football at Brown (1989) and Colorado again (1991-1992), Steckel coached in Denver (1993-1994), Tennessee via Houston (1994-1999)— where he again coached in a Super Bowl (XXXIV)—as well as Tampa Bay (2000) and Buffalo (2003). But perhaps the most important aspect of Steckel's life has been his family:

his wife, Chris, and their three adult children—sons Christian and Luke and daughter Lesley.

While the preceding information may read more like a publicity bio, mentions of those three aspects of Steckel's personal history—the Marines, football and family—provide a template for his impressive leadership credentials. It has been through these diverse experiences that he has come to understand the truth behind the old sports cliché, "Behind every great team is a great coach."

Steckel says he has talked to many coaches over the years, and he routinely asks them about their philosophy. Ironically, they will talk about offensive and defensive schemes, but rarely will they be able to produce a coherent philosophical approach to not just coaching players but teaching them about the important things in life. "As a leader, you know you're going to make mistakes," Steckel says. "You know you're not going to be popular all the time. But you have to know what you believe in."

That's not to say having a game plan is not important. In fact, it's one of the most important aspects of leadership at any level and doesn't just apply to sports but also carries over into business, personal finances, family matters and spiritual concerns.

"Everybody needs a game plan," Steckel says. "Most games are won or lost in the final two minutes of the game. You have to have a game plan, and you have to be precise. A game plan consists of many answers for different situations that may come up in life."

"You must have an attitude of 'what if.' If this happens, what am I going to do?" he adds. "You've got to know the situation, the mission and who the enemy is. The mission of a team is to be successful whether that's in the family, on a sports team or in the Marine Corps. Then you have to have answers for all of those situations."

Steckel points to a number of Proverbs that support his belief in having a game plan, including Proverbs 18:15: "The mind of the discerning acquires knowledge, and the ear of the wise seeks it." True to a coach's form, Steckel has created a game plan that he says will build a championship team or organization. It's a system he refers to as simply "the five Cs: communication, cooperation, contribution, commitment and Christ."

According to Steckel, a solid foundation for any team must begin with effective communication—first from the leader and second within the ranks of the team members. "Communication is of the utmost importance to teamwork," Steckel says. "There are some Marine Corps principles that I have learned—principles that the Marine Corps has used since their inception. They're things like 'Know yourself and seek self-improvement.' I can't really communicate until I know who I am and hopefully how I'm being received. Communication has to be clear and concise, and to some extent it has to be comprehensive."

With great communication, however, comes great responsibility. "When it comes to building a team, you have to communicate well," Steckel says. "But when you communicate, the best coaching pointer I can give someone is to always put yourself in the other person's shoes. If you can do that, you can communicate in a way that you think that person can understand this or receive this or know that this is a genuine concern."

For that to happen, teammates must spend time together and get to know each other. Otherwise, effective, honest communication can't really take place, and the foundational key to teamwork is simply washed away. To describe this concept, Steckel uses the phrase, "Time together equals trust."

"That's a relationship," he says. "It's like a husband and wife. They start out in their marriage, and they're spending time together and learning more about each other. So there has to be that mutual respect. Then as you spend time together, that trust element starts building, and now you've got yourself a great relationship with your wife. The same is true with your teammates or your employees, and now you can go anywhere."

The next step toward building a great team is cooperation. Again, Steckel believes that the team leader or coach is vital for this essential dynamic to take hold. "You have to know your team members and look out for their welfare," he says. "But how do you look out for them? You do things that are going to challenge them. So cooperation to me is team chemistry, and team chemistry is mutual respect for one another. I look at my three children, and I can assure you that I don't favor any of them. I look at them the same. I look at them with mutual respect in the same fashion. I really believe that when you allow people to cooperate, you've got to have good chemistry."

But before cooperation can take place, Steckel believes that trust must be in place. It's that all-important bridge that allows communication to function like a well-oiled machine and not break down in the middle of the journey. In Proverbs 25:19, we are warned that "trusting an unreliable person in a time of trouble is like a rotten tooth or a faltering foot."

"Cooperation is far more than just getting along," Steckel adds. "Denying yourself is a way of cooperating. It's losing yourself for the cause. That's what the Christian faith says. That's what any coach would say to his players on the team. What's the objective here? The objective is to win. Are we going out to play basketball tonight so that your name is in the headlines or that we as a group win the game? So you shouldn't be worried about how many points you score or how much time you played."

When Steckel was the offensive coordinator for the Tennessee Titans during the team's Super Bowl run in 1999, he often encouraged his players to embrace the concept of mutual respect by using a popular leadership quote: "It's amazing how much can be accomplished when no one cares who gets the credit."

That idealistic point of view gracefully merges with Steckel's third C in the list: contribution, or, as the former coach defines it, "developing a sense of responsibility

41

in your subordinates." "How do you allow people to contribute?" Steckel asks. "I couldn't wait for game plan day. I wanted to hear what everybody had to say, because I knew that I didn't have all the answers, and I knew that they had better answers than I did in certain situations. They knew that I'd eventually give them credit—either suddenly or later or momentarily. I wanted them to make a contribution."

This was also true in 2002, when Steckel became a volunteer offensive coach for his son Luke's high-school football team in Brentwood, Tennessee, where he helped lead them to a 5A State Championship.

"Every single player played," Steckel says. "They all played, because I knew the importance of contribution. The number one desire of an employee is to make a contribution to an organization. That's called teamwork.

"If the leader is blind to the importance of everybody being a part of the team and utilizing their gifts and talents that God has given them, he's a terrible leader," Steckel frankly adds. "Most leaders don't look at it that way. Most leaders just want to do their thing. But the leader has to have insight into the skills and gifts that his team has. It's his job to find those things."

But it isn't just on the playing field that contribution is an important element of teamwork. Steckel has also seen this invaluable principle take root in his home life, where—with the support of his wife—he raised three very different children.

"Our family was like a basketball team," he recalls. "My wife was the center. She was the MVP. Everything revolved around her. I was the point guard. That was my contribution. I brought the ball down the court, and I called the plays. I'd give it off to my son Christian who was the shooting guard. He was the oldest. He impacted the other two much like he still does to this day with his observations of life. He was the guy who took some shots. I always called my daughter, Lesley, the power forward because she was the rough-and-tumble one. She's got some fight. Then Luke came along, and he was the other forward. So we had a team and everybody knew their roles."

Once each team member understands and accepts their role, the next step is for each member to make the commitment to excellence and to give it their best. Unfortunately in today's society, the word "commitment" does not have the same power it once did. This is evident in the fact that 50 percent of all marriages don't last. Steckel also points to the increasing variety of scenarios where commitment has fallen by the wayside, such as athletes who refuse to report to training camp and soldiers who go AWOL in the middle of their service to the military.

"People don't understand what the word 'commitment' means. The true meaning is pretty challenging. It's pretty emphatic. But I think people often slide commitment into the promise category."

From a spiritual standpoint, commitment means adhering to the advice given by David in Psalm 37:5 (and then benefiting from the results as described in Psalm 37:6, *NIV*): "Commit your way to the LORD; trust in him and he will do this: He will make your righteousness shine like the dawn, the justice of your cause like the noonday sun."

This passage serves as a connection from commitment to the final *C* in Steckel's five-point plan: Christ. "You must have Christ at the center of your marriage or at the center of your being as a Christian man, as a Christian woman or as a Christian leader," he says.

One of Steckel's favorite Scriptures on this topic is Proverbs 15:33: "The fear of the LORD is wisdom's instruction, and humility comes before honor." On the other hand, Steckel says that selfishness—which is direct opposition to any kind of leadership—can kill teamwork in a heartbeat or slowly over time.

"We as individuals are fighting an incredible, built-in self-centeredness," he says. "We have to fight that every single day. We have to intentionally deny ourselves. But so often we do what we want to do, and we get on a team and do what we want to do. That's where you've got to know the cause. The cause of Christianity is to spread the gospel of Jesus Christ. It's not about you. It's about Him. So when you're on a team, it's not about you. There's too much me, me, me and not enough we, we, we. There's too much showmanship and not enough sportsmanship."

Indeed, great teams require an enormous amount of humility from every single member, including the coach.

This philosophy is birthed from a powerful passage written by the apostle Paul: "Do nothing out of rivalry or conceit, but in humility consider others as more important than yourselves. Everyone should look out not [only] for his own interests, but also for the interests of others" (Philippians 2:3-4).

Embracing this vital teaching allows us to engage in an activity that Steckel describes as "instant obedience." (Read more about this concept in "In His Own Words.") This is exemplified by a willingness to immediately follow orders from anyone in authority and is ultimately keyed by a desire to foster a servantlike attitude within the context of a relationship with Christ.

Jesus Himself said, "If you love me, you will obey what I command" (John 14:15, *NIV*).

Those are strong words coming from the greatest leader to ever step foot on the earth, and they remind Steckel just how important his role of leader as a coach once was and how important his role as the president and CEO of FCA is today.

"When I called plays in the NFL, I always asked the question, 'How do you expect me to control 22 people on the field at the same time?' I can't," he says. "The good news is I know the One who can. That's the One I surrender to and give full control."

TRAINING TIME

1. Steckel used to tell his players, "Let me take you where you can't take yourself." Describe a coach or leader who has improved your skill or talent in some area. What are some tangible ways that person helped you?

2. How important is it for you to have a game plan when striving to reach an individual or team goal? Read Proverbs 16:9 and Proverbs 21:31. How could you apply the concept of having a game plan to your daily walk with Christ and the goals and dreams He has placed in your life?

3. Of Steckel's five Cs—communication, cooperation, contribution, commitment and Christ—which one do you struggle with the most? Why?

4. When talking about teamwork, Steckel often uses the phrase "Time together equals trust." In what ways have you found that the time spent with teammates (or the lack thereof) impacts the end result of the team's efforts? How important is trust when it comes to decisions made in the heat of battle?

5. Steckel talks about "instant obedience" (see "In His Own Words"). Have you experienced this concept in your personal life? Why does instant obedience seem to be such a countercultural idea? In what ways can you surrender to Jesus and His will for your life?

"The only place that you have instant obedience is in the United States Marine Corps. There's no other place in America. Everybody wants to talk, suggest and give their opinion and all that. But in the Marine Corps, if there's somebody over you and he tells you to do something, you don't say, 'Excuse me, sir, have you considered this?' There's a mutual respect for the rank of the Marines; and they know that they've been where you are, and they've been promoted. So there's mutual respect and instant obedience. In Vietnam, there were two cries that you always heard on the battlefield. One was 'Radio operator!' That guy didn't say, 'I'm not going up there.' He was diving right next to that infantry officer and giving him the phone, so he can call his artillery unit or call for air strikes—in the heat of the battle. He doesn't say, 'Well, it doesn't look too good now.' He goes right now—right now! The other cry was 'Corpsman! Corpsman!' That meant somebody was hurt. Somebody was wounded. He didn't say, 'I'm not going out there right now. It's pretty heavy.' He went right then. That's instant obedience. You've got to know your position and your role. There were times I was a colonel in the Marine Corps. There were times I was a second lieutenant, and I just followed orders. But a lot of people don't know their roles on a team. They're the sergeant, but they want to be the colonel."

—Les Steckel

4

KNOW (AND ACCEPT)
YOUR ROLE

Cat Whitehill
U.S. Women's Soccer Team Defender and Olympic Gold Medalist

Now you are the body of Christ, and individual members of it.
1 CORINTHIANS 12:27

I am a member of a team, and I rely on the team, I defer to it and sacrifice for it, because the team, not the individual, is the ultimate champion.
MIA HAMM

Cat Whitehill knows a little something about dynasties. She played for the University of North Carolina soccer program, which through 2007 has accumulated 18 of 26 NCAA titles—including championships in 2000 and 2003 (Whitehill's freshman and senior seasons at Chapel Hill).

Since 2000, Whitehill has been a mainstay on the historically dominant U.S. National Team, which over the last 17 years has claimed two World Cup titles, 3 Olympic gold medals (Whitehill played on the 2004 team, but an injury kept her from contributing to the 2008 team), 3 Confederation of North, Central American and Caribbean

Association Football (CONCACAF) Championship titles and 3 CONCACAF Gold Cup championships.

Even back in her home state of Alabama, she was part of a club team that claimed five state titles, four of them with Whitehill on board. So it's not surprising that Whitehill, a self-proclaimed sports junkie, grew up being inspired by dynasties—even if they weren't always in the same sport. "You look at Michael Jordan and how incredible he was at the game of basketball," Whitehill says. "And then you look at Scottie Pippen and see that he was an incredible player too, but so many people forget about him and Dennis Rodman and Horace Grant and Steve Kerr and B. J. Armstrong. They all made the Bulls become one of the greatest dynasties of my era. None of those players cared that Michael Jordan was as great as he was because Michael Jordan cared about how his team won. That's what makes someone become the greatest."

Born in Virginia but raised in Birmingham, Alabama, Whitehill came by her love of sports honestly. Her father, Phil Reddick, played football at Virginia Tech and would toss around the pigskin with his daughters, Cat and Virginia. But that's not the only way Reddick was influential in Whitehill's life. His roles as associate pastor at Briarwood Presbyterian Church and, more importantly, as spiritual leader of the home played a significant part in her devotion to God.

"Because I come from a Christian family, it was ingrained in my head from day one," Whitehill says. "When

49

I was five years old, I accepted Christ into my life. I remember I was sleeping on my trundle bed one night, and my parents and I prayed together. When you're five years old, you just do what your parents do, and I had different situations where I could've chosen another path, but God just made sense. I've grown in Him, and I came from a Christian school where I received an incredible knowledge of the Bible and the history of Christ."

From the outside looking in, Whitehill admits many are likely to hold preconceived notions about her upbringing. She enjoys busting the myths that for years have accompanied those who grew up in households that were overtly churchgoing and ministry-oriented.

"When you hear that I'm a preacher's kid, you might think I'm the rebellious kind," Whitehill says. "But my family allowed me to choose, and they never forced their views on me. Both my sister and I are so grateful for that, because never once did either one of us stray from our faith. It just clicked with both of us. Obviously, there have been ups and downs in my career and ups and downs in my personal life, but having God in my life is what's kept my head above water."

Whitehill has also benefited greatly from her family's close-knit nature. One of the many lessons she learned from her father was that "you can always help your teammate be better." In fact, Whitehill has grown to love the feeling that comes from helping someone improve in his or her abilities—especially when no one else ever knows.

"Teamwork is putting your personal preferences aside and looking at the person on your right and the person on your left first," Whitehill says. "It's putting aside everything in your personal life and your athletic career and doing whatever it takes to make someone else better. In turn, if you're going to make them better, they have to decide that they want to make you better."

Whitehill admittedly gets frustrated—as an athlete and as a sports fan—when she sees high-profile athletes blatantly put their selfish desires in front of their team's goals. "People describe certain athletes as great team players, but sometimes when the spotlight is shining on you, it's easy to forget about teamwork," Whitehill says. "But it's important to remember that you can't do it alone. When you put others first, it just makes the game a lot more fun, and it makes playing the game a whole lot easier."

While Whitehill was learning the finer art of traditional teamwork at UNC, she met, fell in love with and, on December 31, 2005, married husband Robert. Their venture as a couple has opened her eyes to a whole new element of the team concept.

"I'm not just one person anymore," Whitehill says. "There's a lot more compromise that comes with marriage. I can't just make a decision and have that be the end. I have to go to Robert, and we have to talk it out. It's a great learning experience for me, because I'm a pretty stubborn person. When we come together and make a decision, that's really cool. It's the same thing when you come together as a team, and you make a decision or you win a game. I think you get so much more out of it than if you were to do it by yourself."

The same can be said for Whitehill's involvement on the U.S. National Team. She has learned a great deal about compromise and unity from her vast international experience. Whitehill played for the Under-16 National Team in 1998 as well as the Under-18 squad from 1998 to 2000. She played a key role at the 1999 Pan American Games, leading the U.S. to a gold medal with a spectacular long-distance goal in the championship match against Mexico.

With the Under-21 National Team, Whitehill was a starter and an invaluable contributor as the U.S. squad collected four consecutive Nordic Cup titles from 2000 to 2003 (five consecutive titles, dating back to 1999).

On July 7, 2000, Whitehill made her first appearance on the women's National Team against Italy and has been a contributor as both a starter and key bench reserve ever since. At the 2004 Summer Olympic Games in Athens, she started three of the five games as the U.S. women claimed the gold medal. She also made headlines by filling in for the injured Brandi Chastain during the 2003 World Cup, where the team finished in third place.

"The standard is very high," Whitehill says. "It's high in the way that you play the game. It's high in your mental capacity. The standard is high everywhere. If you were a star in high school and you come to a team like North Carolina or if you were a star in college and you came to one of these national teams, you're going to be humbled. You're not going to be the star anymore."

And even as team oriented as the majority of the national team's athletes have been, there's always the potential for self-serving motives to be lurking around the corner. Perhaps, Whitehill suggests, that's why winning under those circumstances (with the country's elite players all gathered together) is that much more special.

"We're all a bunch of type-A females, but when we compromise and we come together as a team, then we can use our abilities to make the team so great," she says. "It's having the ability but also figuring out that we're a team, and we're not just a bunch of individuals."

Maybe it's because of the way her father ingrained certain principles into her head as she was growing up. Maybe it's because of her passion for college and professional team sports. Or maybe it's because of the personal experiences she has accrued over a lifetime of playing soccer at the highest level. Most likely, however, Whitehill's desire to put the team first in all situations is the result of a combination of all of the above.

"Teamwork has been easy for me," she says. "I just love watching sports, and I love watching the details of sports. I just want to win. I have this strong desire to win. If I need to push my teammates into the goal with the ball, I will do it. I will do whatever it takes. I know I can't do it alone. I want to win so badly that I will do whatever it takes for my teammates to get better."

Arguably, the teamwork concept has not always been emphasized within the walls of most churches. But White-hill believes this foundational principle is clearly taught throughout both the Old and New Testaments. "You can see teamwork throughout the whole Bible," she says. "There wasn't just one disciple—there were 12. Each one had an incredible quality about them. You see the idea of people working together for a common goal all over the Bible, but sometimes you don't think of it as teamwork."

One of the more blatant representations of team-work can be found in 1 Corinthians 12, where the apostle Paul compares the Body of Christ to the human body. In verses 27-31, he addresses the issue of different roles that Christians play in order for the Church to be successful in its mission of bringing the unsaved to salvation: "Now you are the body of Christ, and individual members of it. And God has placed these in the church: first apostles, second prophets, third teachers, next, miracles, then gifts of healing, helping, managing, various kinds of languages. Are all apostles? Are all prophets? Are all teachers? Do all do miracles? Do all have gifts of healing? Do all speak in languages? Do all interpret? But desire the greater gifts. And I will show you an even better way."

Paul is letting all believers know that there is a place for everyone on God's team; and each position, or role, is just as vital as the next. "The bench is just as important as the people on the field," Whitehill says. "I've had a lesson in both. I've been on the bench and I've been on the field. God always has a plan, and whether I'm on the bench or on the field, He wants me to be in that role. For me, the role is important, because I can show Christ through that role. If I'm a bench player, I can be okay with that. It's not where I want to be, but I can push the other defenders and make them better. If their line is off, I can tell them, because I have a much better perspective. If I'm on the field, I want someone on the bench to do the same thing for me."

But true to form, the all-too-common human element of pride eventually works its way into the mix. Selfish motives—whether driven by insecurity or arrogance—cause people (and especially athletes) to question their station in life or on a team. King Solomon wisely pegged this wrong way of thinking in Proverbs 21:2: "All the ways of a man seem right to him, but the LORD evaluates the motives."

"Everyone thinks they should be on the field," Whitehill says. "They don't see through the eyes of the coach or the eyes of their teammates. They see through their own eyes. You're thinking, *I'm better than that player. Why am I not out there?* You're at a competitive level, so you are a great player. But for some reason, there's something that separates someone else from you on that day or maybe the coach just likes them better. There's a lot that comes into play, but the pride issue is huge. For someone who has a lot of pride, if they don't know their role, a lot of times they won't stay on the team."

Overcoming pride takes a solid understanding of who we are in Christ. Philippians 1:6 tells us that "He who started a good work in you will carry it on to completion until the day of Christ Jesus." In other words, anyone who is insecure about his or her ability and feels the need to achieve individual greatness in order to find security and self-worth can trust that our Creator has a plan that no amount of success in athletics or elsewhere can match.

Another great reminder can be found in Colossians 2:9-10: "For in Him the entire fullness of God's nature dwells bodily, and you have been filled by Him, who is the head over every ruler and authority."

Both of those assuring Scriptures help Whitehill stand confident in her faith, no matter what trials she may face on or off the field.

"Knowing who God is and knowing what God did for us is really important," Whitehill says. "It's important to love people in spite of what they may say to you, what they may do to you or who they are and what they believe. That's who Christ was and that's who God wants us to be. My teammates know what I believe, and I know what they believe, and we can still be great teammates. I can still be a witness to them, because I'm not going to back down. I'm stubborn. They're not going to back down either, because they're stubborn; but in the end, it's really Christ who wins."

As important as it is for Cat Whitehill to demonstrate godly teamwork to her teammates and to the greater soccer community and sports world, her desire to exercise this irreplaceable core value is also steeped in a solid understanding of just how powerful a difference a unified, fully functioning group of believers committed to excellence can truly make.

"We're a congregation," Whitehill says. "We are Christ's Body. If we can remember that, teamwork just makes so much more sense. If we realize that we're representing Christ and the pastor is the one in the spotlight, we can just follow them and make the pastor greater, because of how we act and because of who we are as a congregation."

Whitehill says some of her friends often ask why she still plays soccer after all of these years. In response, she usually refers to her love of the team and the love of learning new things on a daily basis. Whitehill also enjoys the opportunity to be a role model for young soccer players and sports fans of all ages throughout the entire country.

"I want them to know that we're not all going to be the Michael Jordans of this world," Whitehill says. "And if you are, the greatest thing you can do for someone is to build them up to be the best that they can be.

"So many people have this perception that you have to be Michael Jordan or Tiger Woods," she concludes. "Yes, they are excelling at their sports, but as humans we can excel to the best of our ability. That's what Christ wants, and that's what's important. That's what a great team wants—to get the best out of each other."

TRAINING TIME

1. Cat Whitehill references Michael Jordan and the Chicago Bulls as one of the greatest examples of teamwork. What are some other dynasties that come to mind? What do you think are some of the key components of a sports dynasty at any level?

2. What are some of the roles you have played on a team? Have you ever felt as if your role wasn't as important as another player's role? Why do some positions in a group dynamic get more attention than others?

3. Read 1 Corinthians 12:12-31, in which Paul compares the Church to a body. In your sport or team dynamic, how would you compare the various positions and roles to the parts of the human body? Have you had to compete or fulfill a task with someone missing? How did that impact the group's ability to succeed?

4. In what ways have you felt called to use your talents and gifts within the Body of Christ? Have you ever felt as if your role was not important or not significant? If so, explain. Read Philippians 1:6. How does this promise from God change any uncertainties you feel about God's call on your life?

5. What does true greatness in the spiritual sense mean to you? What are some ways that you can strive to be a great "teammate" within the Body of Christ?

"My freshman year at UNC was one of the greatest learning experiences for me. I didn't start one game until the national championship game. That was really hard for me, because I came in as a highly recruited freshman. Throughout the NCAA tournament, I was coming in as a sub at forward, but then the coaches started putting me in as defender. I started playing really well, and I was clicking with the backline. Little by little, I gained more playing time, and then one of our forwards was struggling, so the coach decided to put me in. In 2003, I wasn't the starter in the first game of the World Cup, but then Brandi Chastain got injured, and all of the sudden I stepped in and didn't come out for the rest of the tournament. I started out in a completely different role. And in the 2004 Olympics, I was a starter and then all of the sudden I wasn't a starter in the medal round. But I could still cheer on whoever was playing for me. People notice. Even if they don't say anything, they notice. It was hard for me. It wasn't easy. I cried to my family, but I was able to show Christ through that experience and know that God had a plan. I can say that now. It's a lot easier to say it now than it was at the time, but people are watching whether you think they are or not."

—Cat Whitehill

5

TRUST OR CONSEQUENCES

Andy Pettitte
Major League Baseball Pitcher

Never let loyalty and faithfulness leave you. Tie them around your neck; write them on the tablet of your heart. Then you will find favor and high regard in the sight of God and man.

PROVERBS 3:3-4

Men of genius are admired. Men of wealth are envied. Men of power are feared. But only men of character are trusted.

ARTHUR FREIDMAN

Trust is a funny thing. It takes years to build but can be destroyed in an instant. Trust requires honesty, communication, loyalty and proven moral integrity. It is one of the foundational elements behind every great team.

Andy Pettitte knows all about the fragile nature of trust. He has spent his entire life building up trustworthy relationships with his family, his friends, his teammates, the baseball community and the public at large. Yet a single seemingly insignificant misstep can open the door for doubt, which often then results in a certain measure of distrust. In today's society, it doesn't take much for a cynical public (and an even more cynical media) to question one's integrity and chip away at that bedrock of trust.

Pettitte found that fact to be all too true in December 2007 when his name was mentioned in the highly publicized *Mitchell Report*, the written results of an investigation led by former Senator George Mitchell into the prevalence of performance-enhancing drugs within Major League Baseball (MLB). The report and subsequent public statements made by Pettitte revealed that in 2002 and in 2004, Pettitte, in an attempt to recover from elbow injuries, had received injections of human growth hormone.

Even though the use of the human growth hormone was not illegal or banned by the MLB at the time, the onslaught of attention that followed (and the brutally negative reaction by some members of the press) caused the New York Yankees' pitcher to think twice about continuing his career. Was subjecting his family to an invasion of privacy worth it? Was it fair to put his teammates through the media circus during spring training?

Having already signed a contract to play in 2008, Pettitte ultimately had one choice and one choice only. "I felt that [quitting] wouldn't be a very honorable thing to do; that wouldn't be a thing to do as a man," Pettitte told reporters on February 18, 2008. "I felt like I needed to come out and be forward with this. Whatever circumstances or repercussions come with it, I'll take it like a man, and I'll try to do my job."

That's because at his core, Pettitte is the best kind of teammate. He's the best kind of husband and father as well. He is a trustworthy man whose lifelong commitment to integrity cannot be shaken by the overreaction of the vocal minority who are always seeking to make mountains out of proverbial molehills. Pettitte understands that there is no such thing as perfection and that whether people trust you or not isn't always up to you anyway.

Those are just a few lessons about teamwork that he has learned over the years. Originally from Baton Rouge, Louisiana, Pettitte's family moved to Deer Park, Texas, when he was in the third grade. There, his baseball career flourished, and while he was pitching for Deer Park High School, he drew the attention of pro scouts. Although he was selected by the Yankees in the twenty-second round of the 1990 Draft, the towering lefty decided to first attend San Jacinto College in Texas before signing with New York.

Pettitte played in Yankee pinstripes from 1995 to 2003 and was a part of four World Series championship teams. He then spent three years (2004-06) playing for the Houston Astros and led that club to its first World Series appearance in 2005, before returning to the Yankees in 2007.

Considered one of the most dominant postseason starting pitchers in the modern era, Pettitte ranks second among Louisiana-born pitchers in career wins (behind Ted Lyons's 260) and has never had a losing record.

But long before Pettitte was making a name for himself in the Fall Classic, the star athlete's education about teamwork began in a much different setting. Although he was raised in what he describes as a "very strong Catholic family," it was a fateful first visit to the church of his sister's friend that set the tone for his spiritual growth.

"I was 11 years old when I went with her one night," Pettitte says. "It was really the first time in my life that I heard about having relationship with the Lord and heard that I needed Him as my personal Savior. That was the night that I accepted Jesus into my heart and was saved. I've felt like an absolutely different person since then."

About four years later, Pettitte began attending Central Baptist Church—the church that he still calls home today. It was there he met his wife, Laura. She was the daughter of the pastor (since retired), and her brothers were active in ministry there as well. Pettitte would eventually serve in various capacities at the church: teaching in Sunday School, singing in the choir, and mentoring teens, young adults and young married couples.

As a young Christian athlete, Pettitte learned one of the most important lessons about teamwork, not on the baseball field, but in his home and in his church, where strong men of faith taught him that trustworthy relationships are built on integrity.

"My dad was a man who always showed me love," Pettitte says. "It was tough love sometimes, but he always made time for me. If he told me he was going to do something, he would always do it for me. My father-in-law was a wonderful Christian man. He was just constantly in the

Word. When I looked at him, I saw a man who just loved the Bible and was always studying the Word. My brother-in-law worked in the youth department at the church, and I was under him. I was around the Word and I was around Christian people, and these things were just constantly being instilled in me."

Pettitte also says his openness to the Holy Spirit was a key factor in those earliest inclinations toward a lifestyle of godly righteousness. "I was convicted to not drink," he says. "I was convicted to not use the Lord's name in vain. He took all the bad language away from me. I was just extremely convicted of these things at a very young age. I thank the Lord that He's kept His hands around me and protected me. I've had so many people praying for me. I think that's a huge reason why I've been able to live the life that I've lived. God's protection has just been on me."

Pettitte is especially thankful for his wife, Laura, whom he credits for the desire to pursue integrity and strive to be a faithful, trustworthy man. The couple has been acting as a team since they first met as teenagers and made a commitment to abstain from sex until they were married.

Pettitte truly believes that his wife is a mirror image of the woman written about by Solomon in Proverbs 31 and agrees wholeheartedly with verses 10-12: "Who can find a capable wife? She is far more precious than jewels. The heart of her husband trusts in her, and he will not lack anything good. She rewards him with good, not evil, all the days of her life."

Because Pettitte views his wife as a treasure and a gift from God, he has always been conscientious of any actions that could damage the bond of trust they have forged over the years. While many athletes often struggle with the tantalizing temptations that lurk around every corner, Pettitte says that for him the exact opposite has been true.

"It hasn't been that difficult for me, because I have kept myself away from certain situations," he says. "A lot of people put themselves in bad situations; but we're human, and we're going to fall, and we're going to fail. Have there been opportunities for me to screw up? Of course there have. But you don't jeopardize your marriage and that trust. That's the biggest thing for me that I've always tried to do. Again, it's because I've been involved in the church, and I've seen what can happen, and I've seen people's lives ruined if you lose the trust of your spouse. It's going to be hard to get back, and it's hard to overcome. I just thank God that I haven't put myself in those situations where my wife would not trust me or would have doubts about me and my love for her."

While Pettitte doesn't hold an official position at his home church, the unofficial ministry he has done gives him a bird's-eye view of just how devastating those trust-busting mistakes can be on a marriage or in a family or even between friends. He's found this to be especially true when the loss of trust is caused by sexual activity that is contradictory to biblically sound doctrine.

"I think there are a lot of things that are carried into marriages when those individuals have been involved with other people," Pettitte explains. "A lot of people come to me, even though I'm not a minister. I think people know that I'll listen, and they can talk to me. I know a lot of people who have bad stuff going on in their marriages, and it's from things that happened before they were married. You're going to reap from some bad decisions that you make in your life. All of us have made bad decisions in our lives, and usually you're going to reap some of that stuff. That's why it's so wonderful being a Christian, because you can ask God for forgiveness, and He forgives you of it."

As an athlete equally committed to teamwork and sharing his beliefs, Pettitte has found that the trust between him and his teammates often opens the door for him to counsel them on relationship issues. It's a direct reflection of the promise found in Proverbs 3:3-4: "Never let loyalty and faithfulness leave you. Tie them around your neck; write them on the tablet of your heart. Then you will find favor and high regard in the sight of God and man."

"I have a unique opportunity to reach out to my teammates," Pettitte says. "I don't try to judge anybody. I just try to love them and encourage them. I always tell them that when you marry someone, I believe that it's for life. You should stick with your wife and figure out a way to get through it. I believe that's how God wants it, and I believe Satan wants every marriage destroyed and to break every family up. So it's given me a lot of opportunities. As you can imagine, in baseball, a lot of guys are screwing up and doing a lot of wrong things. I try to be as genuine as I can, and I thank the Lord that guys will share stuff with me and open up with me when things happen. I think they just know that I'm going to love them, and I'm going to pray for them."

But none of these opportunities to share God's love with others would be possible if it weren't for Pettitte's desire to emulate Jesus. He understands and embraces the fact that to be a good teammate requires the same level of trust and respect as it does for him to be a good family man and a good friend. His belief is backed up by what Jesus taught in Matthew 5:37: "Let your word 'yes' be 'yes,' and your 'no' be no.' Anything more than this is from the evil one."

Says Pettitte, "Whenever you say you're going to do something, you do it. There are a lot of people in the world today whose word doesn't mean a whole lot. If that's where you're at, then I don't think you're showing a whole lot of integrity. Nobody's perfect, and we're all going to screw up, and we're all going to mess up. But that's how we should try to live our lives. If I tell my children I'm going to do something, I need to be the kind of father who's going to back it up and try to do that for them."

This principle carries over to Pettitte's professional life as well, and in particular is something he strives to

67

maintain when dealing with his team's upper management. At the conclusion of the 2007 season, the Yankees
put a one-year offer on the table for him to return in 2008.
Pettitte, who has struggled with elbow issues for the past
several years, asked for a player's option so that he
wouldn't be forced to make a rushed decision but instead
make a prayerful, wise choice.

"If I had signed a two-year contract with those guys, I
would have felt obligated to come back and play for
them," he explains. "Even if my arm hurt, I would just try
to pitch through the pain. Well, they gave me an option,
which means that if I felt like I was healthy, I could just
activate the option. They trusted my word that if my arm
was hurt, they believed that I wouldn't activate the option just to make the money that they were going to offer
me. The Yankees showed a lot of faith in me with that situation, and I would hope they did that because they
think I'm an honest man and that I would have the integrity to do the right thing. As a man, it made me feel
good that they would say, 'Hey, Andy, we'll entrust this to
you. We'll let you make this decision because we know
you're not going to try to pull something over on us.'"

So when the *Mitchell Report* was released a week after
he signed the contract, it was no surprise that the entire
Yankees organization rallied to support him. When he
met with the media at spring training, he was flanked by
manager Joe Girardi and general manager Brian Cash-
man. Sitting just a few feet away were close friends and

teammates Jorge Posada, Derek Jeter and Mariano Rivera.

Everyone in that clubhouse and in the front office knew that Pettitte's rare lapse in judgment was not a reflection of his character. They knew how important it was for him to have his teammates' trust. The same was also true for his wife, Laura, who stood by his side throughout the entire process as he worked to restore any trust that might have been lost.

And for that to happen, Pettitte will do the same thing he did to build that trust in the first place. He will be a faithful, loyal, moral man and will continue to reflect those values in every area of his life—the ball field, the church and, most importantly, his home. That's how Pettitte plans to maintain his standing as someone who his teammates can count on long after his retirement.

"I'm big on relationships," Pettitte says. "I care about the guys on the team that I play with. I want to try to be a positive influence on my team—not just on the baseball field but in their lives. When I'm done playing and I walk away from this game, I hope that I've impacted somebody's life in a positive way."

TRAINING TIME

1. Have you ever made a mistake that caused someone to lose trust in you? What steps did you take to restore that trust between yourself and others?

2. What role does teamwork play when it comes to trustworthy relationships with a spouse, a family member, a teammate or a fellow Christian? Is it possible to be a successful team without trust?

3. Andy Pettitte says that he has "a unique opportunity to reach out to my teammates." What does their openness to his counsel say about the level of trust they have in his moral integrity? Who are some people that you go to for wise counsel? What about their character makes them excellent candidates for such a role in your life?

4. Pettitte tells a story about a time his team's management trusted him to make an honest and timely decision. Have you ever been in a similar situation? How was your word tested? How did the outcome affect your working relationship with those involved?

5. Read Proverbs 3:3-4. How important are loyalty and faithfulness within any given team dynamic? What are some consequences when those values are absent? What are some ways that you can be more loyal, faithful and trustworthy?

"When I was dating my wife, we made a commitment to one another that we weren't going to have sex until we got married. I don't think people realize how huge a commitment that is, especially with teenagers. But if you commit yourself to not doing that, then you're going to focus on other things in your relationship, and you focus on your walk with the Lord. I don't know where I would be without my wife. My wife, as far as I'm concerned, was the strong one between the two of us—especially back then. My wife was brought up in church. She was raised in church. She was so grounded when I met her—it was unbelievable—whereas I was a new Christian. But hey, I'm a man, and I don't believe I could have done it without my wife. It was a commitment that I wanted to make to her. It was a commitment we both wanted to make. But let me tell you something, if it wasn't for her, I would have messed up. My wife was just so strong and so convicted. It was something that we were able to do together. It didn't matter to me that we didn't have sex before we got married, because I loved her, and I knew that's who I wanted to spend the rest of my life with. But as a man, I don't know if I could have done it if I hadn't been in a relationship with a woman like my wife."

—Andy Pettitte

6

EYES ON THE PRIZE

Luke Ridnour
NBA Guard

*One thing I do: forgetting what is behind and reaching forward
to what is ahead, I pursue as my goal the prize promised by God's
heavenly call in Christ Jesus.*

PHILIPPIANS 3:13-14

*Destiny is not a matter of chance; it is a matter of choice. It is not a
thing to be waited for; it is a thing to be achieved.*

WILLIAM JENNINGS BRYAN

If you've never heard of Coeur d'Alene, Idaho, don't feel
too badly. Even National Basketball Association (NBA)
point guard Luke Ridnour, the town's most famous product, wouldn't expect many people to know much (if anything) about his birthplace.

Even though its population is anything but tiny (as
of the 2006 census, there were a little over 41,000 inhabi-
tants), only those living in the northwestern United States
tend to know much about the city that sits along the edge
of the scenic Coeur d'Alene National Forest. And it was in

Coeur d'Alene that Ridnour first fell in love with the game of basketball. He lived there until he was seven years old and recalls attending a Christian school where his mother was a teacher.

"When I was in kindergarten, my dad used to play basketball with me at lunchtime against the third and fourth graders," Ridnour says. "That was my first memory of playing basketball. He was a coach, so he would come in and mess around with me and play two-on-two against the other kids."

Oddly enough, Ridnour and his family went even deeper into obscurity when they moved to Blaine, Washington—a town with a population under 4,000 that sits in the state's extreme northwest corner and rests against the U.S.-Canadian border. While there, he attended Blaine High School with about 400 students and graduated with 90 seniors. The tight-knit community was extremely supportive of its athletic programs, which Ridnour led to a pair of state hoops titles. More important for him, however, was the development of his ideas about teamwork.

"Since I can remember, it was that same crew of guys playing together," he explains. "It was never about putting one guy in front of another guy. It was always about our team. We represented that community, and we weren't just playing for ourselves. That's the coolest thing I can remember—the loyalty we had toward each other. We didn't care who the star was. We just wanted to be there for each other and win."

73

Ridnour credits his father for providing the earliest lessons about teamwork. Rob Ridnour coached high-school basketball (including his son's team) before taking over as the head coach of the International Basketball League's Bellingham Slam. It was the elder Ridnour who instilled in his son some of those fundamental concepts about teamwork, such as sharing the ball and looking out for one another.

"The biggest thing my dad taught me about teamwork was that everyone should stick together through thick and thin," Ridnour says. "These are the guys you're going to be with, and no matter how bad it might look at times, that's your crew that you've got to pull together with. The guys who are on the court are the ones who have to get the job done. You can't look to other people. You've all got to do it together."

While pursuing his NBA dream, Ridnour says that maintaining a relationship with Christ was rarely a priority. He grew up in church, but his focus on athletics deterred him from taking a serious look at the faith his parents embraced. Still, he knew something was missing in his life. "As much success as I'd had, I wasn't very happy," Ridnour says. "I still didn't have very much peace about who I was. But once I hit college, God really spoke to my heart. He started drawing me closer and closer to Him. I started to find peace, and I got excited about the fact that I wasn't just a basketball player, but I was friends with Jesus. That's what really changed my life."

At the University of Oregon, Ridnour found strength and accountability in a group of freshmen teammates who were all experiencing similar spiritual growth patterns. They met together for Bible studies with team chaplain Keith Jenkins—a pastor from Eugene, Oregon—and faithfully attended a local church.

Ridnour says that fellowship opened his eyes "to the power of God and how real He is." Likewise, a growing comprehension of the Bible enhanced his understanding and appreciation for the concept of teamwork.

"It's very much biblical with principles such as putting others before you," Ridnour says. "I think that's what teamwork is. A good teammate puts others before him. No one person thinks they're bigger than they really are. The Bible just reinforced the belief that I can't put myself above anybody else."

Ridnour is especially inspired by the words of the apostle Paul found in Romans 12:3: "For by the grace given to me, I tell everyone among you not to think of himself more highly than he should think. Instead, think sensibly, as God has distributed a measure of faith to each one." "I think that's huge for teamwork," Ridnour says. "A lot of times, you can be worried about yourself and your success. But when you put your team's success ahead of your success, good things happen."

Ridnour earned Pac-10 Player of the Year honors as a junior in 2002-03 and then made an early departure for the NBA, where he was the fourteenth overall selection of the Seattle SuperSonics. After five seasons with the Sonics (a franchise that has since moved to Oklahoma City), he was traded to Milwaukee in a three-team, six-player deal. His experiences at the highest level of competition continue to bring revelation about the biblical principles of teamwork—despite the fact that so much of playing in the NBA is about the individual athletes and their desire to earn high-dollar contracts.

"But no matter what level you're at, the most important thing is still the team," Ridnour says. "My first responsibility is to make sure all of my decisions are going to help the team win the game. The second thing is making everybody else better. It's doing the little things like getting the ball into the right hands at the right time or even scoring at times when you have to."

As a point guard, another line item on Ridnour's checklist is taking care of the ball. And while he agrees that he needs to do everything he can to limit turnovers, he also says that he must avoid the trap of thinking too much about it. "You can't be afraid to make mistakes," Ridnour says. "If you look at some of the great point guards, they were never afraid to take a risk on a pass. For me, being a point guard also means showing your creative side and having the freedom to go out and do what God's called me to do and have fun doing it. I don't really worry about turn-overs. I know it's an important part of the game, but as you play more, you get more confident and don't turn the ball over as much."

For Ridnour to be truly successful at his craft, he must have impeccable vision, or what others often refer to as court awareness. He needs to hone that innate ability to see the big picture and all of its finest details. "For me, good vision is about instinct," he says. "It's about knowing your teammates: what they can do and what they can't do. It's also about knowing the game. When I'm leading a fast break, I have a good idea of where everybody is at, and they might not even be there yet. Then you just let your instincts take over. When I try to force it, that's when turnovers happen. But when you let your instincts go and play freely, you might not see it, but it happens."

Ridnour equates his vision as a point guard to his vision as a follower of Christ. He fully understands the vital nature of having a clear picture of God's will for his life and the ultimate prize that comes with a personal relationship with Jesus. But as a young athlete, Ridnour admits that until he reached college, he didn't always have the vision necessary to see what was around him. He didn't realize what kind of impact he could have on others as a man of faith.

"When God started to open up my eyes and let me see things through His eyes, I could see that there were so many people around me who I could touch," Ridnour says. "It's a daily thing. You can influence and touch so many people just by being around them and saying the right things and being there for them. We get so caught up in day-to-day stuff, but as far as eternity is concerned, we need to keep our eyes on the big picture. So when adversity comes, it's really not that big of a deal when we look at what we have coming."

For Ridnour, this promise for the future is found in Philippians 3:20-21: "Our citizenship is in heaven, from which we also eagerly wait for a Savior, the Lord Jesus Christ. He will transform the body of our humble condition into the likeness of His glorious body, by the power that enables Him to subject everything to Himself."

Having that knowledge of eternal glory along with the understanding that we can have a vibrant relationship with Jesus in this lifetime has helped Ridnour grasp the more personal aspects of teamwork—even as it relates to interactions with his peers off the court. "One of the biggest things a point guard needs to do is have relationships with his teammates," he says. "Whether they're your kind of people or not, it's important not to just get along but to have a sincere relationship with all of the players and coaches. That makes a difference on and off the court. On the court, it's our job to make everybody better and to do that they need to listen to you and respect you."

It took Ridnour a little bit longer to learn how that truth applied to his fellowship with believers. He admits that he once had tunnel vision and would think of himself long before he would think about others. Then he came across the admonition found in Galatians 6:2, where Paul tells us to "carry one another's burdens; in this way you will fulfill the law of Christ."

"One of the things I used to find myself doing in prayer was only praying about my needs," Ridnour re-members. " 'Lord, I need this. Lord, I need that.' But God calls us to pray for all the saints. We're supposed to pray for our spouses, our families and our friends. We're sup-posed to pray for the salvation of people around us. And once you find yourself praying for other people, you start to see your own prayers answered."

From there, Ridnour began to get a clearer picture of what teamwork should look like within the Body of Christ. He made rich discoveries within the pages of God's Word, including a promise given by Jesus in Matthew 18:19-20: "Again, I assure you: If two of you on earth agree about any matter that you pray for, it will be done for you by My Father in heaven. For where two or three are gathered to-gether in My name, I am there among them."

"The Church is one body," Ridnour says. "The Church isn't made up of one person. It's a body of people that goes out into the world. Two or three are so much stronger than one, even in prayer. When you have more people on the same page together, it's much more powerful than when there's just one." This realization has pushed Ridnour and his wife, Kate, to get more involved in their local church and to find time for Christian fellowship. When the couple makes decisions, they ask others to help them pray before-hand. It's been an incredibly enlightening experience and has opened their eyes to the mighty force that is unleashed when biblical teamwork is engaged.

"The Church is the place where everyone *should* pull together," Ridnour expounds. "Everyone has the same common goal. Everyone has the same prize in sight. When everyone is on the same page and everyone has the same vision and can see the same things, it makes it easier to guard against all of the attacks that the devil throws at you. Working as a team, the Church can be a bigger force. It's like we're on a big battlefield and when we're all together, we're much stronger."

The Old Testament gives us many examples of people working toward a common goal. In one such story told in 2 Chronicles 28–31, God's people suffered through the ungodly rule of King Ahaz before his death opened the door for King Hezekiah. In order to bring the nation back to the Lord, Hezekiah began a long, arduous process that included cleansing the Temple, renewing Temple worship, celebrating Passover and removing all of the idols brought in under Ahaz's rule.

The key to Hezekiah's success in restoring the people to God is found in 2 Chronicles 30:12: "The hand of God was in Judah to give them one heart to carry out the command of the king and his officials by the word of the LORD." In other words, the nation had to come together and work as a team with one purpose in mind.

As a lifelong athlete, Ridnour has seen what happens when that singular vision isn't in place. "The worst that can happen in a locker room is when you have fighting going on," he says. "It makes it real tough. When there's no team unity, there's a lot of bickering and people talking behind each other's backs. That's not fun to be around. It's tough to win that way."

Ridnour's assessment lines up perfectly with Proverbs 29:18, where Solomon warns, "Where there is no vision, the people perish: but he that keepeth the law, happy is he" (*KJV*).

"When we're not together, it allows Satan to pick his way in," he adds. "If he can get one person going the wrong way, it just breaks everyone up. That's something we have to be careful about."

In that sense, Ridnour agrees that all believers at some level need to become spiritual point guards. We must all have a sense of our surroundings but never lose sight of the big picture. And that means building and nurturing friendships with the people that are pressing toward the ultimate prize—a relationship with Jesus both here on earth and forever in heaven.

"When you have people around you who are on the same page, you have that accountability that you need," Ridnour concludes. "You've got someone watching your back. It's easy to get sidetracked, and when you try to go solo, you might start doing things you shouldn't be doing. But when you have that fellowship of people and close friends who have the same vision with you, it makes it a lot easier. You know those people are there with you in the battle, and they're with you for the long run."

TRAINING TIME

1. Can you remember the very first team you were a part of? What was your role, and how did you contribute? What lessons did you learn in your earliest experience with teamwork?

2. Luke Ridnour talks about Oregon's success during the 2002 NCAA Men's Basketball Tournament (see "In His Own Words"). Can you think of a time when your role on a team decreased so that the team's success could be increased? How did that make you feel at first? Read Romans 12:3. What can be taken from this passage to help you deal with such scenarios in the future?

3. Read Philippians 3:12-14. According to this passage, what are some qualities associated with good vision? How does knowing that you "have been taken hold of by Christ Jesus" make you feel? How does that promise impact your ability to focus on the prize?

4. How would you describe the perfect teammate, co-worker or friend? What challenges have distracted you from fulfilling that role in the lives of others?

5. Read Proverbs 29:18. In what ways can you apply this verse to the team dynamic? What are some of the ways that you could promote a like-minded vision within your team?

"Sometimes guys that have poor vision are selfish, and sometimes that's just the way they play. They're out to score or maybe they have tunnel vision. If you don't have good vision, it makes it tougher for people to want to play with you. Everyone likes to play with someone who shares the ball. Sometimes there's a need for guys to go and score the ball, but we always like to play with guys who give it up and move the ball around. A lot of it goes back to the 'I' stuff. They always say there's no 'I' in 'team,' and that's really true. That's a huge thing that hinders teams from having a common vision. You look at all of the teams that win, and everyone's involved. Everyone's touching the ball. My sophomore year at the University of Oregon is probably my best example. We had a lot of seniors, and then we had a lot of young guys who were freshmen and sophomores. Those seniors just accepted us. They didn't care how much they played. They just wanted to win. That was one of the most unselfish things I've ever seen, and it carried over to those who were playing a lot. I'll never forget that about our team. We went to the Elite 8 that year and probably the biggest reason we did was because of those seniors supporting everyone who was playing. They put themselves at the back of the bus and put the team first."

—Luke Ridnour

7

Checks and Balances

Curtis Brown
NHL Defender

*Watch out, brothers, so that there won't be in any of you an evil,
unbelieving heart that departs from the living God. But encourage
each other daily, while it is still called today, so that none of
you is hardened by sin's deception.*

HEBREWS 3:12-13

*I urge all Christians not only to attend church services regularly
but also to establish small groups of other Christians to whom
they are accountable. I've seen this simple practice work wonders
in my own life. In fact, I would never have developed real
Christian maturity merely by staying home, reading religious books
and attending church once a week—no more than an athlete
can develop by shooting baskets alone in the driveway.*

CHARLES W. COLSON

It's usually a good rule of thumb to stay away from
stereotypes and cultural clichés in order to avoid potentially embarrassing confrontations with the obligatory
"exception to the rule." But in Curtis Brown's case, even

he admits that a predictable portion of life in Saskat-chewan—his native Canadian province—can be described in two words: *farming* and *hockey*.

Born in the small rural town of Unity, Brown grew up on a farm where he instinctively fell in line with the majority of his young friends. "What Canadians do is hockey," Brown says. "I was probably about four when I started skating. I was just like the other kids. If you didn't play hockey, you were definitely an outsider."

However, while hockey was an unmistakable passion, the thought of a career in the sport was, strangely, the furthest thing from Brown's mind or that of his buddies. "Other than cheering and looking up to these sports heroes, the only thing I was thinking about as a kid was going out in the front yard or down in the basement or out on the ice to play hockey," he says. "You just went out and did it for fun. Never did you think, *That's exactly what I want to do, and nobody's stopping me.* It was more about a love for the game."

His love for the game, however, eventually opened the door to opportunity and at the age of 15, Brown moved away from home to pursue hockey at the Triple-A midget level. The quantum leap landed him four hours from home in Moose Jaw, one of the larger cities in Saskatche-wan, where he played one season before spending a year in Major Junior Hockey.

"Either you grow up quick when you move away at 15, or you never grow up," Brown says. "If you ask me now if I would let my three boys move away at 15, it would be a tough decision, because I know what I went through. You go and live with a host family, but they usually just let you do your own thing. You have a bed there, and they feed you, but other than that you're on your own. That's kind of a young age to be on your own. You grow up quick."

At the age of 18, Brown was drafted by the Buffalo Sabres in the second round of the NHL draft. In his only game with the Sabres that season, he scored a goal and tallied an assist. He spent the balance of the 1994-95 campaign back in Moose Jaw and the Western Hockey League (WHL). Brown was especially busy during the 1995-96 season, spending a brief time with Buffalo along with elongated stints in Moose Jaw and Prince Albert (also part of the WHL) and by helping the Rochester Americans claim the American Hockey League's Calder Cup.

After splitting time between Buffalo and Rochester during the 1996-97 campaign, Brown finally experienced a breakthrough in 1997-98 when he played 63 games for the Sabres. He remained a mainstay at the center position until he was traded to the San Jose Sharks late in the 2003-04 season.

The next year, due to the NHL lockout, Brown played for a minor league team in San Diego before spending 2005 to 2006 with the Chicago Blackhawks and the following two seasons back in San Jose. Following the Sharks' appearance in the 2008 NHL playoffs, he inked a contract to play with the Kloten Flyers in Switzerland's National League A.

While Brown's successful professional hockey career can be neatly summarized into a pair of tidy paragraphs, his spiritual journey is slightly more complicated. "I didn't grow up in a Christian home," Brown says. "It was a good home, but I can count how many times I went to Sunday School. I knew a little bit about who Jesus was and the Christian faith, but I really didn't know anything. I didn't live it. If you would have asked me if I was going to heaven or hell, I would have said heaven more out of hope than knowledge."

Brown attended a Catholic school and by default made regular visits to Mass, where he observed something quite peculiar. His peers who went to the altar for prayer were also the wildest partiers during the weekends. "It never made sense to me," Brown says. "I don't know why that stuck so vividly in my memory, but I was like, *Man, there's more to Jesus and what He did and there's more power in this than what I'm seeing here.*"

Until then, Brown didn't have a living, breathing example of God's grace in action. That all changed when he first arrived in Buffalo, where he met veteran goaltender John Blue. Having previously played for the Boston Bruins and nearing the end of his 10-year career, Blue had an enormous impact on Brown's life—first by his actions and later with his words. "For the first time in my life, I saw a Christian guy who was different," Brown remembers. "He just didn't talk about it. He wasn't always telling me what I needed to do. It wasn't preachy. He just went out and lived it. In hockey, there's not that many Christians who are living it, and here was the first guy I could watch. I could watch his marriage and watch his family. I'll never forget it. He was different."

Blue, now retired from hockey and working in pastoral ministry, was also the first person to demonstrate the significance of the Holy Spirit working within a believer's life. Brown also finally understood the greater purpose behind the Crucifixion and the Resurrection.

"We all mess up. We all screw up," Brown says. "That's why we need Jesus. But there's also a power that allows you to rise up and be stronger than giving in to every temptation and falling down every day. John Blue was the first guy I saw who demonstrated that."

Blue's quiet approach eventually gave way to a conversational style of evangelism. When Brown opened the door of his heart, his elder teammate was ready to lead him to Christ. That's when the real challenge began.

"Right at that point, there was a crossroads—not only in my faith but in hockey," Brown says. "It was kind of scary—especially at that time. There weren't many Christians in the game, and there had been a stereotype that Christians are soft and can't play in this league. People just have a wild and weird idea about what it means to be a Christian. They never open up the Bible and read what David did to Goliath or about what Samson could do.

"I'm a better player today because I'm a Christian," Brown continues. "I'm a better teammate. I'm more responsible. I prepare better. I'm accountable to God, which is a much greater level of accountability than just trying to perform for people. But it was basically taboo to be a Christian. I had heard stories where guys were basically put in the minor leagues or not given a chance because they were Christians."

Brown openly admits he was fearful of what might happen to his career or how his teammates would respond to his open profession of faith in Christ. He was 21 years old and in just his second full NHL season. But Brown maintained a profound and steadfast understanding of the fact that his relationship with God was much bigger than hockey.

"Sure enough, the next day in the locker room, the guys were all over me like clockwork," Brown reflects. "It was basically the moment of truth when I had to stand up and just say, 'Yeah, I'm different now, and this is who I am.'"

Like many players before who had confessed Jesus as their Savior, Brown had to withstand a healthy dose of ridicule and a steady stream of skepticism. His teammates had seen it all before—the zealous new Christian busts down the locker-room door to profess his faith only to fall prey to temptation days, if not hours, later.

But Brown's determination to stay true to his commitment had an unexpected and much-welcomed effect on the other players. "They'll test you for a while," he says. "But when they realize you're the real deal, the crazy thing is people would think these guys would be your nemesis, but once you prove yourself true, they become your protectors. They knew there was something different about me."

What Brown feared might create a wedge between him and the rest of team ultimately pulled them together. It was an incredible picture of teamwork, a concept that ironically has its roots in the Bible.

"Everything we talk about, everything we experience—whether you admit it or not—the Bible is the handbook for life, and it's in there," Brown says. "You can find it in there on any topic. As far as teamwork is concerned, it starts right in the beginning of the Bible with God and the Holy Spirit and Jesus in the creation story. There's teamwork there. They were creating things together."

Few if any will argue against the importance of teamwork within the context of team success. Rarely will a group of individuals playing for selfish interests (no matter how talented they may be) find itself in a position to win championships. But according to Brown, one of the most important intangibles every good team needs is accountability—the willingness to take responsibility for individual or collective actions—which goes deeper than any superficial attempts at team building.

Accountability can also be defined as open and honest dialogue within any given relationship in which the people involved (whether they be family, friends or team-mates) can discuss each other's deeds, motives and per-sonal choices should they be perceived as negative or potentially harmful.

"The best teammates are the guys who are account-able to you and you're accountable to them," Brown says. "Nobody's going to be perfect, but when you know you're accountable to someone and they're accountable to you, it's amazing how much more time and focus and energy you're going to put into the job that you have to do. You don't want to let that other person down."

When accountability is discussed, terms similar to those usually reserved for a peer-to-peer relationship are used. The best example of such a relationship is a close friendship between two individuals who are keenly aware of each other's strengths and weaknesses, each other's tri-umphs and failures. More importantly, this type of bond will foster confrontational communication (when neces-sary) and brutal honesty at all times, both of which are tempered by love and mutual respect.

Brown's first introduction to accountability came through his former teammate John Blue, but he later dis-covered many supporting truths in the Bible. First Thes-salonians 5:11-12 says, "Therefore encourage one another and build each other up as you are already doing." He-brews 3:13 likewise instructs us to "encourage each other daily, while it is still called today, so that none of you is hardened by sin's deception." James 5:16 takes it another step further, telling believers to "confess your sins to one another and pray for one another, so that you may be healed." The writer of that passage clearly understood how difficult it is to maintain a poker face when all of the cards are on the table. But as Brown has experienced firsthand, those who hold tightly to their hands are usually bluffing.

"There are some guys in the league—just like in their personal lives—who don't want to be accountable to anybody," Brown says. "Those guys are the worst teammates, because you can't trust them. Hopefully, my teammates can trust me. But there are some guys who you don't know what they're going to do or what they're thinking. I've played with those types of guys, and that makes it tougher to have teamwork."

Another aspect of accountability is found in the relationship represented by any given hierarchy. The leader may be a coach, a pastor, a corporate president, a business owner or a team captain. The follower may be an athlete, a church member, a board member, an employee or a teammate. No matter what the position or station in life, the proper model for accountability can be found in Hebrews 13:17:

> Obey your leaders and submit to them, for they keep watch over your souls as those who will give an account, so that they can do this with joy and not with grief, for that would be unprofitable for you.

As Brown has seen parallel growth in his career, his family and his faith, accountability has been an invaluable part of the equation. But he has also come to realize that without accountability to God—first and foremost—the other areas of his life simply won't be as successful.

"Your most important team is your relationship with God," Brown says. "In marriage, for example, who is the most important? Well, it's my relationship with God because He's the one who created me. He's the one who's given me His daughter to take care of. The kids are His—He's given me the opportunity to be a steward of them. At the end of the day, He's not only the One who gives me breath every day, [but] He's also the One who can help me and guide me through the other aspects of my life. If He's number one, then I'm going to have a far better chance."

Brown's philosophy is certainly backed up by the Scriptures. In fact, some of his favorite Bible passages serve as stark reminders of the believer's need to be honest with the all-knowing Creator. Romans 14:12, for example, says, "Each of us will give an account of himself to God." A similar truth is revealed in Hebrews 4:13, a passage that reminds us how "all things are naked and exposed to the eyes of Him to whom we must give an account."

That understanding of God's omniscience and the eternal consequence of our actions should alone push us to true accountability with Him. Even at the most basic level, accountability improves the quality of life—that is, if you accept the wisdom found in the Proverbs. In

Proverbs 12:1, Solomon writes, "Whoever loves instruction loves knowledge, but one who hates correction is stupid." He later adds in Proverbs 25:12 that "a wise correction to a receptive ear is like a gold ring or an ornament of gold."

Still, accountability is something that eludes most people. Brown has found that to be especially true in the NHL, where teams are made up of individuals representing a broad range of ages, cultures, social backgrounds and religious expressions. And when accountability is lacking—or in extreme cases nonexistent—the impact on a team can be devastating.

"It pulls the team apart," Brown says. "I think the more accountable players are to one another, the tighter the team becomes. You see that in relationships and marriages. But when you just have people going in their own direction and not falling under that umbrella of accountability, it definitely makes it difficult for everyone to be on the same page."

As far as Brown is concerned, the benefits of accountability far outweigh any perceived loss of personal freedom. On the contrary, there is great freedom in knowing that we have accountability with people who care about our well-being and that we have even greater blessings by allowing God to be involved with every aspect of our lives.

"There's a set of standards that God places on us when we make the decision to follow Him," Brown says. "God isn't just about giving you a free trip to heaven.

That is part of what God has for us, but there's a whole other aspect, which is the Lordship aspect. We need to fall in line and make Him Lord and listen to what He has to say."

TRAINING TIME

1. Curtis Brown says that teammate John Blue was his first example of authentic Christianity. Who was the first person to model the character of Christ in your life? How did that person's example change the way you viewed spirituality and faith?

2. Who are some people who have authority over you? Do you generally agree or disagree with their leadership? How do you usually handle any disagreements with authority? Read Hebrews 13:17. Why is it important to obey and respect those in authority over you?

3. Read 1 Thessalonians 5:11-12 and Hebrews 3:13. What are some of the benefits that come with encouraging relationships? What happens when those kinds of relationships are absent from your life? What are some ways you can encourage or build up your friends, teammates, family members or coworkers?

4. Read Proverbs 12:1 and Proverbs 25:12. What is one of your most embarrassing stories about being corrected or disciplined? How do you feel when someone corrects your mistakes?

5. Read Romans 14:12 and Hebrews 4:13. What are some ways you can use brotherly and sisterly accountability here on earth to prepare you for the day on which you must give an account of your life to God?

"When Jeremy Roenick was playing in Chicago, their captain was Dirk Graham. They'd just finished a period, and the team came into the locker room. Dirk came in, and he looked at one of the assistant captains, Steve Larmer, and he said, 'Larms, don't you care about me?' And Larms said, 'Yeah, why?' He was a little befuddled at why he would be asking that. And Dirk said, 'I just played the worst period. I was terrible out there, and none of you guys said anything. None of you guys said to wake up or pick it up or anything. You guys just let me play terrible like that.' If we're really accountable to each other, we'll say things that need to be said—even if it's not positive—in order to get each other on the right track. We need to have people around us who we can trust— not just to yell and scream and be negative, but to point out the truth. That's what we need in sports and in life. It's biblical. Rebuke is the greatest thing to a wise man. Some accountability groups are just people patting each other on the back. But that's not the whole picture. The truth also has to come out. That's real accountability. It's not a bad thing when people are telling you that you need to shape up. The scary thing is when that voice goes away and people aren't telling you those things because obviously they don't care anymore."

—Curtis Brown

8

TWO-WAY STREET

Sam Hornish Jr.
NASCAR Driver and Former IRL Champion

Just as the Lord has forgiven you, so also you must [forgive].
COLOSSIANS 3:13

*Respect your fellow human being, treat them fairly, disagree
with them honestly, enjoy their friendship, explore your
thoughts about one another candidly, work together for a
common goal and help one another achieve it.*
BILL BRADLEY

Jo Ellen Hornish has a love-hate relationship with auto racing. She's been a huge fan of racing since her teenage years. It's the part where her son Sam Hornish Jr. drives in one of those cars at speeds of 180 to 200 miles per hour that she's not crazy about. "She would have much rather I become a pastor," Hornish Jr. says. "I'm pretty sure of that. There's never been a time where she's said, 'Man, I'm glad he's a racecar driver.' But she knows that it makes me happy."

In reality, Jo Ellen only has herself to blame. Well, herself and her husband, Sam Hornish Sr. After all, it was her son's desire to get behind the wheel that directly attributed to the life-long devotion to auto racing that both she and her husband share. In fact, one of their first dates was to go to an IndyCar race in Milwaukee, and when Jo Ellen was eight months pregnant with Sam Jr., the married couple attended the Indianapolis 500. According to the younger Hornish, the love affair goes even further back than that.

"My grandfather took my dad to the Indianapolis 500 when he was 10," he says. "That sparked my dad's interest in racing. My dad probably would have wanted to be a racecar driver if he ever would have had the opportunity, but he got married right out of high school and never had that chance. So I was into racing at an early age. All of our vacations as a kid were going to races."

Many of those trips were to Indianapolis, which was roughly three hours from his hometown in Defiance, Ohio. He also recalls longer drives—to Michigan and even West Coast swings through California and on to Phoenix. Ultimately it was the appeal of open-wheel racing that drew Hornish into the sport, but it was his family's trucking business that first taught him the concept of teamwork.

Hornish grew up on 40 acres of farmland and lived two miles from his family's church. His father owned and operated a trucking company that dispatched 175 trucks across the United States. The younger Hornish started out as a truck washer and then graduated to the fabrication shop at age 16. After finishing high school, he continued to work in the family business until he won his first IndyCar race—a success that Hornish attributes to the concerted effort of his entire family.

"You hear so many times about how racing has created a lot of victories for people but also a lot of heartaches," Hornish says. "I've been very lucky that my racing has created very little heartache. The worst I've ever been hurt is when I broke my foot. We've a lot of fond memories around racetracks—either when I've been racing or when we just went there as fans. It's been a pretty good ride for us. We've had our family arguments and disagreements along the way, but we've really had a pretty blessed ride. We've had a lot of good things happen."

Sam Hornish Jr., born in 1979, apparently is a master of understatement. He, in fact, has carved out quite a career for himself since first racing at the age of 11 in go-karts. By the age of 14, Hornish was one of the top drivers in the World Karting Association, where he continued to make waves through 1995. After a successful stint in the United States F2000 Series, he joined the Toyota Atlantic Series and won the 1999 Rookie of the Year honors.

In 2000, Hornish received his first big break—an opportunity to race in the Indy Racing League (IRL) with PDM Racing. A year later, he moved to Panther Racing, winning back-to-back IRL championships in 2001 and 2002. Hornish switched teams again in 2004 and drove for the legendary Roger Penske. By 2006, he had set a new IRL record by picking up his third championship. That season was especially memorable thanks to an improbable win at the Indianapolis 500, which he won on the last lap.

"When I started racing, our goal was just to go to Indianapolis and qualify," Hornish says. "We thought that would be plenty enough. We've continued to have that philosophy. We're thankful that we've made it this far, and if you wake up tomorrow and it never happens again, then you accomplished your lifelong dream [from] when you were a kid. So to be able to do so much more in IndyCar—to win races and to win championships—all of that has been a bonus since I made my first start in Indianapolis."

By 2006, Hornish was toying with the idea of making the leap to stock-car racing. He ran two races in the Busch Series (now Nationwide Series) in 2006 and seven races in 2007. Hornish also competed in two Nextel Cup (now Sprint Cup) races in 2007 before making the jump to NASCAR full-time in 2008 for the familiar Penske Racing team. And while the cars may be vastly different, he says the teamwork aspect is virtually unchanged.

"When people think about teamwork, a lot of times, people think about football or basketball," Hornish says. "In most cases, people won't think about racing as a teamwork sport. That's probably because the driver gets about 99 percent of the credit. But racing is probably one of the most teamwork-oriented sports. As the driver, yeah, I have to drive the race car, and I have to make the right decisions on the track. If I do everything perfect out there, we can win. If I don't do things right, we're not going to win.

"As much as I get credit for those things and as much as I get paid, there's as much pressure on the guy that's working 80 hours a week in the shop," he adds. "He never gets his face seen, and he doesn't get paid nearly as much. There are thousands of bolts and fasteners and moving parts on the race car that have to be right if I'm going to have a chance to win. Everybody's got to do their job. The driver's got to do his job. The crew chief has to do things right. The pit crew has to make the right decisions. All the way back to when the car is being built, those things have to be put together right. There are so many things that can take you out of a race. It's very much a team sport."

And teamwork doesn't just happen on race day. It's happening throughout the weeks leading up to the big event. For instance, every race team has several cars that are being worked on constantly—from the engine setup to the paint scheme. The pit crew has daily practices while the marketing team seeks more sponsorship money. Even when the driver isn't meeting with the crew chief and the engineers to discuss mechanical and handling issues, he or she is likely out making appearances to make the sponsors happy.

It all comes pretty natural to Sam Hornish Jr., who says his church background in Ohio taught him a lot about the importance of teamwork. His grandmother picked him, his sister and two cousins up for Sunday School and Wednesday-night services at the local Brethren Church, where he was baptized at the age of nine.

"I always enjoyed going to church," Hornish says. "I still enjoy it now—even the chapel services we have on race weekends. It's nice to be able to focus your attention on something else besides racing. We've got so much pressure on us to go out there and succeed. It's nice to be able to do one thing—whether it's 15 minutes or half an hour out of your entire weekend—and to be able to focus on something else besides racing. It's a nice release from worrying about everything else."

One thing he learned in Sunday School was how Jesus' disciples worked together as a team. As described in Matthew 4:18-22 and John 1:35-51, each of the 12 men had different roles and diverse personalities—a lot like what Hornish has experienced working with various race teams over the years.

He's also been able to temper disappointing team results by taking a look at the big picture and realizing that having a bad day on the racetrack isn't the end of the world. This philosophy was especially put to the test on April 27, 2008, when Hornish and his #77 Mobil 1 team struggled greatly in the Aaron's 499 at Talladega Superspeedway. After a solid start, a vibration in one set of tires forced him to make two pit stops. That misfortune was followed by a blown tire, which put the team down two laps, followed by engine troubles that effectively ended their chances for a good finish.

Prior to the race, Hornish had sat in on a Motor Racing Outreach chapel service and listened to chaplain

Lonnie Clouse talk about the Bible story of Job. "Job was covered in boils from head to toes," Hornish says. "He lost all of his family and all of his property. Hopefully, I don't have to go through anything like that; but some days you sit there, and all of these things are going wrong in racing. You don't think you're going to turn the corner. But then you hear a message like that, and you realize it's not that bad."

Of all the variables that go into teamwork, Hornish says communication is probably the most fundamental and therefore one of the most vital. This proved especially true in his earliest transition from open-wheel racing to stock-car racing. "Everything I've known since I started racing has been about Indy cars," Hornish says. "If the car wasn't right, I knew what to tell them to make it better. Now, I don't know everything about the cars. There's got to be a lot of communication. If we have a condition where the car is pushing or it's loose, I have to be able to communicate that to the rest of the team."

His desire to learn—and do so through communication—is fortified by a number of King Solomon's nuggets of wisdom. For instance, the passage found in Proverbs 15:32 tells us that "anyone who ignores instruction despises himself, but whoever listens to correction acquires good sense." But that doesn't make communication any easier. Hornish has found it difficult in times when problems continue to pop up, a scenario that often creates frustration and tension within the team setting.

"You're always trying to make the car better throughout the race," Hornish says. "You're communicating what you think needs to happen but sometimes it just doesn't get better. You feel like you're constantly falling behind and that you can't keep up with the changes. Sometimes it's hard to keep your head about you and say, 'That didn't work—how about this?' There are a lot of people who lose their head and make more mistakes because that communication is lost. Everyone's speaking English, but something's getting lost in the translation."

In times like that, Hornish extols the virtue of patience, even though raising one's voice or simply shutting off the lines of communication may seem to be the easy way out. "It's tough sometimes, because you know that everyone is trying their hardest," he says. "Sometimes it's very difficult to tell someone they're totally off base. For me being a young driver in my stock-car racing career, it's hard for me to take that stance. But sometimes you just have to get to that point."

And that means admitting mistakes, even if it's Hornish himself who is the person on the wrong end of the stick. "I make hundreds of mistakes every time I go out there and race," he says. "It's the guy who makes the least mistakes who's going to win the race. It's not the guy who's perfect, because nobody's perfect."

For teamwork to flourish, Hornish says there must be an environment of open, honest two-way communication that is grounded by a strong commitment to forgiveness.

The perfect model for this concept can be found in Colossians 3:12-15:

> Therefore, God's chosen ones, holy and loved, put on heartfelt compassion, kindness, humility, gentleness, and patience, accepting one another and forgiving one another if anyone has a complaint against another. Just as the Lord has forgiven you, so also you must [forgive]. Above all, [put on] love—the perfect bond of unity. And let the peace of the Messiah, to which you were also called in one body, control your hearts.

"Being a good teammate is being able to forgive your fellow teammates for making mistakes," Hornish says. "It's also wanting to work hard so you don't let them down; and knowing that if you do make a mistake and you're working as hard as you can, you're going to be forgiven of that."

And while communication with all team members is important, there is a special bond between the crew chief and the driver. Throughout the week, these two must talk about everything from race strategy to car-related issues. During the race, the crew chief alerts the driver to his surroundings with the help of a spotter and verbalizes the game plan at every stage.

"The communication between the driver and the crew chief is extremely important," Hornish concurs. "There've been days in the past when I could walk in and say three words about what the car's doing to the crew chief, and then he's going to make three changes to the car and make it twice as good as it was. That relationship—and that understanding—that a crew chief and driver have is the most necessary component for a successful race team."

In a lot of ways, the relationship between the driver and the crew chief is a lot like our relationship with God. Daily communication helps prepare us for any challenges headed our way, and while living out our seemingly ordinary lives, we can rely on His gentle direction and correction to make good choices and rebound from poor decisions. And while Hornish says he's never woken up in the morning and felt like God was telling him exactly what to do, he does believe that God speaks to him through both wide-open opportunities and closed doors. Psalm 37:23 backs up this concept: "The steps of a good man are ordered by the LORD, and He delights in his way" (*NKJV*).

"Sometimes you don't understand why the crew chief is doing what he's doing, but at some point in time, you've got to trust him enough to make that decision," Hornish says. "In the same way, God makes the right decisions for us, and sometimes He challenges us. The biggest thing is being open enough and smart enough to trust what He's telling you to do, no matter the situation at hand."

TRAINING TIME

1. Think of a bad day that you had recently. What were the circumstances that made that day so challenging? How did the bad day you were having impact your ability to communicate with others?

2. Sam Hornish Jr. says the story of Job helps him to keep his racing trials in perspective. How did Job's troubles impact his communication with his friends, his family and with God? How would you handle the same kind of troubles that Job experienced?

3. Read Proverbs 15:32. Can you describe a time when you ignored some good advice? Who are some people that have given you good advice? How did listening to that wise counsel impact your life?

4. Read Colossians 3:12-15. What are some of the ways this passage tells us we should treat our teammates or friends? How would exercising these values improve communication within a team dynamic?

5. Sam Hornish Jr. shares a story about his former car owner Roger Penske (see "In His Own Words"). What role did trust play in his success at the Indy 500 in 2006? In what ways can the relationship between a driver and his crew chief be compared to the relationship between you and God? What are some ways that you can improve your communication with Him?

"During my Indy Car career at Penske Racing, Roger Penske called all of my races. In 2006, we went to Indianapolis and qualified on the pole. On our last pit stop, we had a problem. The fueling mechanism got stuck in the car. When [the crewman] tried to pull it out, it got stuck and broke off. We had to do a drive-through penalty and fell half a lap behind the leaders. So Roger says, 'If it stays green from here on out, everyone else is going to have to stop again. All you need to do is save fuel and stay ahead of the leader. We're going to be looking good.' As much as I wanted to be upset, I just said, 'That's the plan, and we're going to make that plan work for us.' Some of the cars started to pit, but then a car got into the wall and brought out the caution. Eventually, a couple more cars had to pit, and we ended up ninth in line with four laps to go. A few more breaks went our way here and there, and we ended up winning the race. We didn't end up making the pass for the win until right before the finish line. Everything happened when it needed to, and Roger's communication kept me calm and made sure I didn't get upset and make a mistake. It enabled us to win that race—the biggest win of my career."

—Sam Hornish Jr.

9

All for One

Tamika Catchings
WNBA Forward and Olympic Gold Medalist

The body is not one part but many.

1 CORINTHIANS 12:14

They said you have to use your first best player, but I found out you win with the five that fit together best.

RED AUERBACH

When Tamika Catchings was in the third grade, she played on her first basketball team alongside sister Tauja. Her father, Harvey Catchings—an 11-year NBA player—was the coach of the squad that, other than his daughters, consisted of boys. The fact that Catchings and her sister were the only girls on the team is an interesting fact, but it's not nearly as telling as the principles they learned from their dad's coaching style. "We had to learn how to play as a group," Catchings recalls. "My dad always preached about how it was a team effort. We got that drilled in our head."

Maybe that's why Catchings, the All-Star forward for the WNBA's Indiana Fever, has never really struggled with the concept of teamwork. No matter how much individual success she has accrued on the basketball court, her number one goal has always been winning and doing it as a team.

Catchings was born in Stratford, New Jersey, in 1979 while her father was playing for the New Jersey Nets. He had previously played in Philadelphia. When he was traded to the Bucks, the family followed him to Milwaukee, where he played five seasons. When he played one final NBA season with the Los Angeles Clippers, the rest of the family remained in Milwaukee before moving to Italy, where he continued his career.

Tamika Catchings attended first grade at an overseas international school but moved back to the Abilene, Texas, a year later, where she attended second grade. She then moved to Chicago where she lived through her sophomore year in high school. During that time, her parents divorced, and she and her siblings stayed with their mother.

In Chicago, her athletic career started to blossom. As a sophomore in 1995, she was on Stevenson High School's Division AA State Championship team and was named Illinois Ms. Basketball. The following year, her mother moved the kids to Duncanville, Texas, where, as a senior, Catchings led Duncanville High School to a state title.

By then, the recruitment letters were steadily streaming into her mailbox. But as early as the eighth grade, Catchings had developed a strong desire to play for the University of Tennessee, after happening to notice Lady

111

Volunteers' head coach Pat Summitt on a nationally tele-
vised game.

That's when everything changed.

In Knoxville, Catchings was an instant star. As a
freshman, she played a key role on the team that went 39-
0 en route to the 1997-98 NCAA national championship.
By the time her college career was over in 2001, she had
become just the fourth woman to be named First Team
All-American in four consecutive seasons.

But her newfound national fame within the world of
women's basketball wasn't the only major change in
Catchings's life. She also found herself straying from
some of the good habits she had learned as a child and
teenager. "We grew up in the church," Catchings says. "Everything the church offered, we did. Our parents just made
sure that we were always involved in some positive activity. Even though we got older and may have fallen off as
far as going to church and doing the things we had grown
up doing, we always ended up going back to it."

Admittedly, though, Catchings mostly neglected her
spiritual needs during her first three years in college—
that is, until she tore the anterior cruciate ligament in her
right knee against Mississippi State on January 15, 2001.

"After I got hurt my senior year in college, it seems
like my need for a relationship with God became that
much more obvious to me," Catchings says. "There was a
huge chunk that was missing in my life that I was filling
with basketball. Basketball was my god. Before the injury,

I couldn't go to church because I had practice, or I had something else going on. I started to lose that balance that I grew up with. So after my injury, I got back to going to church; and then one thing after another, my faith continued to grow. It is who I am, and that's how I've come through adversity, knowing that I have Him to count on. It makes things that much easier."

Her renewed commitment to Christ also helped her solidify the true meaning of teamwork, which she had been taught at a very young age. "Teamwork is a group of people who come together to work for a common goal," Catchings says. "Whether it's winning a championship or whether it's getting a project done, they have a common goal, and everybody's on the same page."

As part of Tennessee's national championship team, Catchings caught her first glimpse of selfless team play. She shared the court with future WNBA stars Chamique Holdsclaw and Semeka Randall (now an assistant coach at West Virginia University), yet each of those top-tier athletes put aside their personal goals and worked to fulfill one singular vision. "All of us came together," Catchings says. "Some people had to sacrifice more than others, but we did it together as a team. It's not like one individual did it for the whole team."

Catchings says that the same was especially true of the amazing collection of athletes who made up the gold medal-winning women's basketball teams at the 2004 Summer Olympics in Athens and the 2008 Summer Olympics in Beijing. Both squads went undefeated thanks to some of the greatest female hoops stars to ever grace the basketball court, including Lisa Leslie, Diana Taurasi, Tina Thompson, Sue Bird and Kara Lawson.

"You get the best players in the U.S.A.," Catchings says. "All of us on our respective teams are the best players. You go from our teams in the WNBA to practicing for a few days and then winning a gold medal. People had to put aside their differences and understand that it's not about them. It's not about the Indiana Fever or whatever team they play for. This is about us getting together to win the gold medal, and that's what we did."

Sadly, those displays of true teamwork are not always prevalent, and many times individualism rises up and destroys chemistry between teammates. Catchings lists pride, ego and a general inability to accept one's role as some of the primary enemies of teamwork. Ultimately, however, she believes that modern society's love affair with pop culture and fame may just be the biggest culprit.

"In this world, people put superstars on a pedestal—the rich, the famous, the sports stars," Catchings says. "So we're taught from a young age, 'That's who I need to be.' There are players who accept their roles, but there are a lot of players who want to be 'the woman' or they want to be 'the man.' That's where you struggle with teamwork, because you have players on the team who don't grasp the fact that they could win more games if everyone would just do what they're good at instead of trying to do everything."

Found on the reverse side of that coin is the dynamic created by athletes who covet more playing time, more recognition or more respect. The desire is usually internalized at first, but if it is left unchecked, resentment will eventually bubble over into the locker room and have a potentially devastating impact on the rest of the team. For those struggling with the temptation to give in to that negative dynamic, Catchings has a simple solution.

"Work harder," she suggests. "Don't sit there and blame somebody else for what they're doing. You always hear the story about people who say, 'I'm waiting for God to do something in my life' while they're sitting on the couch at home. It's hard for God to make a move if you're not putting out the effort."

Another enemy of teamwork—which often accompanies individualism and is the root cause of covetousness—is jealousy. As Catchings has witnessed firsthand at various levels of competition, the words written in James 3:16 are all too true: "For where envy and selfish ambition exist, there is disorder and every kind of evil."

"Jealousy can destroy a team," Catchings says. "A lot of it comes from outside people saying, 'You can do this and you can do that' or 'The only reason you can't do it is because that other player is getting two more shots than you are.' It's funny when you think about it, but that happens, and then you start buying into it; and you start saying, 'Yeah, I should be playing more.' But whatever God has for you, you will have. Nobody can take that away."

115

It is Catchings's confidence in who she is and, more importantly, in who she is in Christ, which allows her to stay shielded from jealousy, self-serving individualism and prideful behavior that so predictably ravage the team concept. Her assurance can be traced back to the powerful passage found in Jeremiah 29:11: "'For I know the plans I have for you'—[this is] the LORD's declaration—'plans for [your] welfare, not for disaster, to give you a future and a hope.'"

Even with that understanding, Catchings admits struggling with one of the more seemingly innocuous—though nonetheless deceptive—enemies of teamwork. Because of the high expectations that are placed on her as one of the WNBA's elite players, she must always stay alert to the danger of trying to do too much to help make up for what others aren't getting done.

"Sometimes when you try to cover up for other people's weaknesses, you end up doing more and more and more," Catchings says. "You look at Michael Jordan. When he started playing, he was doing everything. But once he figured out how to let his teammates help him, he won six championships. There's a fine line between trying too hard and not trying hard enough."

Like Jordan, Catchings has experienced a great deal of individual success in the professional ranks. After sitting out the Indiana Fever's 2001 season due to an injury, she returned in 2002 and won WNBA Rookie of the Year honors. In 2005, she scored her 2,000th point in the WNBA, reaching that mark faster than any other player had ever done in the league's history. Catchings also reached 1,000 rebounds, 400 assists and 300 steals faster than any other WNBA athlete. Catchings has won a pair of Defensive Player of the Year awards (2005 and 2006) and was the leading vote-getter for the 2006 WNBA All-Star Game.

Still, with all of those personal accolades and individual achievements, Catchings is most interested in team success and that elusive WNBA Championship. In order for that to happen, she understands how important it is for the team to recognize the truth found in 1 Corinthians 12:12-14, where the apostle Paul compares a physical body to the Body of Christ. In verse 12 of that passage, he explains that "as the body is one and has many parts, and all the parts of that body, though many, are one body—so also is Christ." He continues in verse 14 with this nugget of divine wisdom: "So the body is not one part but many."

"I can't win every game by myself," Catchings says. "The more that my teammates can do, the better off this team will be. When I can help somebody else and they can get a little bit of love, I don't care who scores the most points per game. At the end of the game, if we won and you scored more points than me, that's great."

Catchings has also learned that there is a rewarding aspect of teamwork that many people tend to overlook. Romans 12:10 says, "Be kindly affectionate to one another with brotherly love, in honor giving preference to one another" (*NKJV*). It's that last phrase, "giving preference to one another," that really stands out to Catchings who—despite her knack for scoring lots of points—truly enjoys seeing her teammates shine.

"It's all about spending that extra time after practice with players who need to work on certain things," Catchings says. "I haven't always been a great communicator, but in becoming a leader for my team, it's like, *What can I do to help people?* The biggest thing for me is just constantly being in my teammates' ears—telling them what we expect from them and telling them what we need from them. Knowing that, I think any player will play better."

One of Catchings's favorite examples of teamwork in the Bible can be found in the lives of the 12 men that were called to be Jesus' disciples. This diverse group quickly learned that they were no longer looking out for their own self-interests but, as it says in Philippians 2:4, "for the interests of others."

"That's a huge step," Catchings says. "They were so close to God, and as disciples they had power to do so many different things. But at the end of the day, to be able to carry out His will and to be able to work together as a team, that's kind of awesome to think about."

When Catchings talks about the importance of serving within the confines of the team, she isn't just giving lip service or saying what people expect her to say. She has backed up her desire to lift others up to a higher understanding of teamwork through her Catch the Stars Foundation. The organization was birthed on the heels of a series of successful "Catch the Fever Camps" and "Catch On to Fitness Clinics."

"Our mission is to help kids catch their dreams one star at a time," Catchings says. "We have a mentoring program. We have a fitness program. But one of the things we always come back to is being able to work with other people. We put kids together who have never been together in their life. While they're at the camp, they're going to learn to work with that team and that person.

"You have to teach these things to kids at an early age," Catchings adds. "You look at these role models these days, and a lot of the athletes are not doing the positive things they should be doing. Even if you don't think people are watching, they're always watching."

Catchings believes that teamwork must eventually go well beyond the sports realm and carry over into every aspect of life—especially for those who have made the decision to accept Christ as Savior and Lord.

"There are so many people out there who challenge the Word," Catchings says. "They challenge Christianity. They challenge whether there's a God or not. That's why there are so many other religions, because people are looking for something else. That's why it's important for us to come together and unite. We need to gather as Christians. Our main goal is to praise God and to live our lives for Him and to please Him. It's not to please man, because like it says in the Bible, if you try to please man, you're always going to be disappointed."

119

TRAINING TIME

1. Have you ever been on a team on which everyone was relatively equal in their level of talent? If so, what challenges did that present to the concept of teamwork?

2. What are some messages in our society that promote selfish ambition? Read James 3:16. What are some ways jealousy and selfishness can cause disorder and evil within a team's ranks? Have you ever dealt with a similar situation? If so, what did you do to overcome the strife caused by these negative attitudes?

3. Catchings says that she enjoys watching her teammates excel. Read Romans 12:10. How does this attitude contrast with what you usually see exhibited by today's superstar athletes?

4. Read Philippians 2:1-4. What does the apostle Paul say are some key values necessary to keep a team focused on one goal? How should the admonition of verses 3 and 4 play out on the field or at work? How does the concept of putting others first translate to your role as a member of God's team?

5. Read John 13:35. According to Jesus, what is the significance of godly teamwork as it relates to reaching your world? In striving to live this teaching out in your life, what characteristics of Christ will you begin to pray for?

"Eighth grade was the first time I ever saw Pat Summitt. I was flipping channels, and I saw her flash across the screen. For whatever reason, she just caught my attention. So I watched the game for a little bit; and I thought, *If I ever get good enough to play for her, that would be a dream come true.* Coach Summitt was everything I needed in a basketball coach at that time in my life. Pat taught her players that becoming a great player is one thing, but just becoming a better person is the most important thing. It's not just about who you are on the basketball court. It's about becoming a well-rounded person—having respect for yourself, having respect for others and living life to the fullest. She also taught that you ride or die as a team. When people got in trouble, she would punish that individual person, but she would punish the whole team too. Some people don't agree with that, but I think it held us accountable. If you're going to be a great team, you've got to have accountability. You know that if you do something wrong, you're not just affecting yourself; you're affecting the whole team. We learned to have love for one another. We're teammates, and the relationships we built in college—no matter what team you're on—you can either build positive relationships or bad relationships. It's hard to play on a team with people who don't like you."

—Tamika Catchings

10

THE TIES THAT BIND

Mark Knowles
*Former Men's Doubles Tennis Champion of the U.S. Open,
French Open and Australian Open*

*Do to others what you would have them do
to you, for this sums up the Law and the Prophets.*
MATTHEW 7:12, *NIV*

*The only society that works today is also one founded on mutual
respect, on a recognition that we have a responsibility collectively
and individually, to help each other on the basis of each other's
equal worth. A selfish society is a contradiction in terms.*
TONY BLAIR

Most historians believe that modern tennis emerged
sometime around the mid-1850s and was based on a similar French game that was invented as far back as the
twelfth century. Since that time, the sport has evolved at a
rapid pace. From a greater emphasis on power to the size
and consistency of the racquets—outside of the rules and
prevailing etiquette—there isn't much left today that re-
sembles the original discipline. Maybe that's why doubles
tennis is so intriguing. There's something about it that

makes you wonder if that's how the game used to look and feel—with a high value placed on serving and volleying, finesse and creativity.

Those are the reasons Mark Knowles loves doubles so much, because in essence he's a throwback to the past—and in more ways than one. And even though his original plan was to be a successful singles player, his old school leanings eventually prevailed.

"I had a decent singles career there for a while, but I really flourished on the doubles court," Knowles says. "Part of that is probably because my game is more suited for doubles, but I also like having a partner. Baseball has always been my favorite sport, and I also thought it would be great to be part of a team. I just like the team camaraderie. Having played doubles the last few years, I like winning together and losing together and going through life's experiences with somebody else. It's pretty cool.

"I think that comes from playing singles for so long and the fact that the tennis circuit is a pretty lonely world," he adds. "Everybody realizes that it's glamorous when you make it, but as it is in any sport, there's usually a lot of hard work and a lot of remote places and hard, lean times that you have to go through in order to get to the finish line. Maybe doubles has allowed me to enjoy it more. It's not as lonely."

Knowles was practically born with his appreciation of teamwork on the court. Born and raised in the Bahamas, he grew up in the shadows of two parents, Vicky and

Samuel, who were skilled tennis athletes in their own right and worked together teaching the sport. In fact, Knowles's mother (the former Vicky Rees of Great Britain) was a professional tennis player who played in Wimbledon and was close friends with the likes of legends Fred Stolle and Rod Laver.

"I grew up around tennis and just fell in love with it right away," Knowles says. "I probably had a racket in my hand at three years old and always had great dreams to be the best player I could be. The nice part growing up was that [my mother] was friends with all of these people that I looked up to growing up. That was a unique perspective at a young age to be able to be around people like that and talk to people like that. I think it helped with my tennis development."

When Knowles was 10 years old, he was invited to attend the Nick Bollettieri Tennis Academy in Bradenton, Florida, where he trained alongside such future stars as Andre Agassi, Jim Courier and David Wheaton. As he stepped into this brave new world, Knowles brought with him a foundation of faith that was rooted in his home country's strong Christian convictions. Growing up in the Bahamas, he went to church and attended Sunday School every week.

While most people would probably assume that his separation from that world would have weakened him spiritually, it was at the tennis school where Knowles began forging his own desire to learn about God apart from the habits that had been ingrained in him back home. "There was a gentleman by the name of Chip Brooks," Knowles recalled. "He and his family went to church every Sunday, and he spurred on my spiritual emphasis. We had FCA meetings every Wednesday night, and there were a lot of us who were trying to learn a lot more about our faith and what our purpose was on this earth. In a selfish world and in a tennis world where everyone's so focused on the means to an end, it was nice to take a step back. It allows you to stay grounded and not be quite so insulated when you're in the tennis world."

But when Knowles accepted an offer to play tennis at UCLA, his relationship with Jesus took a backseat. There wasn't the same level of accountability there. Balancing an NCAA Division I athletic career with the academic rigors of one of the nation's top universities jumbled his priorities somewhat. Knowles achieved All-American honors in both singles and doubles but lagged in his quest for spiritual growth.

When Knowles entered the professional tennis world in 1992, he chased success as a singles player but quickly realized that doubles was going to be his ticket to a lengthy career. Along with long-time partner Daniel Nestor of Canada, Knowles reached the finals at the Australian Open in 1995 and the finals at the French Open and the U.S. Open in 1998. The duo finally broke through for a taste of Grand Slam glory in 2002 with a victory at the Australian Open. After reaching the Wimbledon final that same year, they went on to capture the U.S. Open title in 2004 and the French Open title in 2007. Before Knowles and Nestor parted ways in 2007, the team was consistently ranked among the top five in the world and had spent some of that time in the number one spot.

Amid his rise to doubles prominence, the five-time Olympian was still searching for the deeper meaning of life. True purpose eluded him. But that all changed when Knowles met his wife, Dawn, a native of Little Rock, Arkansas. The two were married in 2003 and have since added two children to their family. They split time between Dallas, Texas, and Nassau, Bahamas, while making sure that Christ is at the epicenter of everything they do.

"I was fortunate to meet my wife, who had a very strong faith," Knowles says. "She reenergized my faith, and that allowed me to take a step back from the tennis world and remember to give thanks and to continue doing the little things that make a huge impact. So since I met her, we've really tried to devote ourselves to God."

Knowles now enjoys added depth and greater perspective to his already strong grasp of the teamwork concept. "My faith has allowed me to take every individual for who they are," he says. "We're all different. We all have our shortcomings. We all sin. None of us is perfect, and I think the biggest principle is to treat others like you want to be treated."

Knowles's philosophy is an indirect but intentional take on Matthew 7:12—also known as The Golden Rule—

in which Jesus instructs us to "do to others what you would have them do to you, for this sums up the Law and the Prophets" (*NIV*). It's also the key ingredient to one of teamwork's most fundamental elements: respect. Knowles wholeheartedly believes that this irreplaceable product of genuine love and concern can be the difference between success and failure.

"For me, respect means you're allowed to mention little imperfections or give constructive criticisms without the other person feeling like it's a personal onslaught and vice versa," he says. "That only comes with mutual respect. Whether it's your playing partner or your wife, when they're pointing out something that you can improve, it's because they're on your side. They want the best for you. It's not like they're trying to put you down and make themselves better. They're just trying to make the unit better, and I think that applies to doubles tennis just as it does personal relationships."

But unlike modern society's definition of respect, which is so often only performance based, Knowles says respect is more about the commonalities that all humans share—we are all God's creation and deserve to be treated with dignity, compassion and empathy. "I think that when you have a strong relationship with God and you have a strong faith, it allows for the imperfections of others a little bit more," he says. "Maybe you have a greater flexibility in understanding other individuals. We're not all the same. Most great marriages are two completely different people,

127

but when you put them together, they make a great unit. Just because somebody doesn't experience the same emotions or act the same way or respond the same way as you do, that doesn't mean you can't succeed together."

But respect doesn't happen overnight. There are several steps that one must take in order to foster respect for others and to gain that same level of respect in return. "The biggest thing is communication," Knowles states. "Sometimes that's not easy. Some of my mixed doubles partners don't speak English as their first language. Then it's about emotions and trying to read the other person's body language and do things that will allow them to relax and feel comfortable and flourish.

"When there isn't a language barrier, it's about being up front with each other and really communicating," he continues. "Sometimes it's about tapping into each other's personalities. Some people are very guarded and quiet, and some people are outgoing and maybe borderline obnoxious. But whatever the case may be, those two individuals have to be tied together to make it really successful."

If respect laces together the initial strings of teamwork, then perhaps genuine care and concern for each other is the double knot that makes that bond nearly inseparable. "When someone else sees that you care about their feelings or their emotions or their results, then they think, *Wow, this person genuinely cares about my well-being*," Knowles suggests. "We're fortunate enough to play a sport for a living, which is pretty cool, but it gets intense sometimes. We all get down after losses. We all get disappointed when things don't go well. We're all super competitive. The things that make us successful can also unravel us. That's why it's always nice to have an encouraging and caring group of people around you—whether that's your peers, friends or playing partners."

And with a mutual respect that is fortified by love and compassion, the by-product is often a group of people who will lay it on the line for one another because they know the same effort will be returned. "There's a sense of accountability there," Knowles says. "You don't want to let down your partner. You want to be there for him or her. That's the great thing about being a team. You try to reach that extra level that you want to attain. You know the prize is out there, and you want to share it together. I think I've gotten better at that as my career has gone on. Early in my career, I wasn't as aware that there were other people out there. You're really caught up in yourself. You're not really concerned about anyone else. But I think my emotions have been enhanced by playing doubles."

One of Knowles's secrets is the ability to read his playing partner's body language and then turning what he learns into an appropriate action. It might mean giving words of encouragement to lift his partner's spirits, or it might mean guarding his tongue in order to not bring him down. "Some people can play great on a team and not get along that great," Knowles says. "But I'm the kind of guy who prefers to be friends and get along with

129

my partner. To do that, you've got to do things with them. You've got to make an effort. You can't shut them out and lead your own personal life and only look at things from your perspective. I think it's important to look beyond that and try to see things from their angle."

Knowles was challenged to obey his own rules of relationship when Nestor secretly worked out with a new partner before abruptly leaving Knowles after the 2007 U.S. Open. It wasn't just about tennis. It was about a long-standing friendship that had endured some downs but was mostly full of ups. "Our families were very close," he says. "Both of us were in each other's weddings. It was a pretty deep friendship. In our game, you have changes. If you want to change, you usually do it at the end of the season and give the other guy a chance to get another partner. But he just left me high and dry. He had a partner, and I didn't have anybody."

Despite the shocking breakup, Knowles did his best to bless Nestor and release him to his new venture. For the remainder of the 2007 season, he forged short-term partnerships with the likes of Jamie Murray, Fabrice Santoro and James Blake, with whom he reached the finals of the Davidoff Swiss Indoors tournament. Knowles has now joined forces with another formidable doubles player, India's beloved Mahesh Bhupati. But before closing the book on the Knowles-Nestor era, the veteran Bahamas Davis Cup team member welcomed his old partner back for one last tournament.

The team's championship effort at the season-ending 2007 Tennis Masters Cup not only brought closure to the situation, but it also allowed Knowles to extend grace to Nestor and stay true to Jesus' teaching found in Luke 6:27-31: "But I say to you who listen: Love your enemies, do good to those who hate you, bless those who curse you, pray for those who mistreat you. If anyone hits you on the cheek, offer the other also. And if anyone takes away your coat, don't hold back your shirt either. Give to everyone who asks from you, and from one who takes away your things, don't ask for them back. Just as you want others to do for you, do the same for them."

Certainly Knowles wouldn't classify Nestor as his enemy, but he still found that the situation compelled him to follow Christ's example and forgive him and leave the offenses in the past. Knowles is ever aware, however, of the daily struggle to respect one another. "It's especially true in today's age with terrorism and the advancement of technology," Knowles says. "Our world has gotten pretty crazy, but you look back in the Bible, there are stories that make me think maybe our stories aren't that different. There's a general lack of respect from human being to human being. You see that today with all the violence. There's definitely a lack of compassion today. But it needs to be the first thing we think about. "That's why it's so important for the Church to work together. That's why Christians need to have that trust in each other and respect for each other, so the world will be drawn to God's love."

131

TRAINING TIME

1. What societal changes over the last 60 years have contributed to the world's view of teamwork? What elements of teamwork still hold true today? What are some positive examples of teamwork that you have witnessed or been a part of recently?

2. Who are some people you have a great deal of respect for? Why? What attitudes or personality traits tend to hinder your ability to respect those around you? Read Matthew 7:12. In what ways do you think this verse promotes the concept of mutual respect?

3. What are the differences between how you respond to someone you respect and someone you don't respect? What do you think are the root causes for your reactions to those two types of people?

4. Can you describe a recent time when a teammate or peer showed you genuine care and concern? How did that affect your ability and desire to work together?

5. Have you ever been hurt by someone you respected? How did that situation impact your ability to respect others? Read Luke 6:27-31. How does this Scripture line up with the way you dealt with the person who hurt you? In what ways do Jesus' words contradict the world's philosophy on forgiveness and on the loss of respect in the world?

"Midway through the 2007 season, my doubles partner, Daniel Nestor, dropped me for somebody else. It was one of those things where not only were we a great team and we had a great partnership, but we also had a great friendship that I thought was pretty special. We had committed to play together for the entire year. He had talked about us finishing our career together because we were both winding down to the end. We were still doing very well. The worst part for me, though, was he went out and found a new partner without ever letting me know. I think I've gotten a little bit wiser with age. Maybe if it had happened earlier in my career, I might not have handled it as well. But it's one of those things in life. You really learn that no matter how much you have things figured out, life sometimes throws you a curveball. I didn't see that coming, but at the end of the day, it's not a huge thing. Nobody died. It's just sports. I'm also a believer that things always happen for a reason. I thought Daniel and I had something great going. We had a chance to continue a great legacy that we had established. But as one door closes, another one opens."

—Mark Knowles

11

Soaring with Eagles

Steve Fitzhugh
Former NFL Safety and National Spokesperson for One Way 2 Play—Drug Free

*Do not be mismatched with unbelievers. For what partnership
is there between righteousness and lawlessness? Or what fellowship
does light have with darkness?*

2 Corinthians 6:14

*When you choose your friends, don't be short-changed by
choosing personality over character.*

W. Somerset Maugham

When Steve Fitzhugh picks his friends, he does so very
methodically, carefully and selectively. There are certain
qualities he looks for in people, and he takes an almost
formulaic approach to all potential relationships. And he
teaches others to do the same.

For instance, Fitzhugh says the primary quality of a
close friend is that he or she is like-minded in his or her
faith. The individual must have accepted Jesus as his or
her Savior and must have made a long-term commitment
to following Him. But that's just the beginning of Fitz-

hugh's laundry list, which also includes trust, confidence and character.

"I don't have to watch my back with them," he says. "They're confident enough in themselves to encourage my success. I don't want to hang around someone that's hatin' on me. I want to hang around people who want me to be a champion. I don't want anybody around me who's looking for opportunities to bring me down. I want somebody who's looking for opportunities to build me up and encourage me to be a success."

Fitzhugh doesn't take his choices lightly, because he hasn't always had much of a choice at all. Growing up in Akron, Ohio, the former NFL safety with the Denver Broncos didn't get to pick his family, his neighborhood or his environment. His world was punctuated by drugs, alcohol, cigarettes, physical and verbal abuse, and the divorce of his parents when he was about seven years old. Fitzhugh lost his 60-year-old mother to a cancer linked to her 40-year smoking habit.

"I saw all of the bitterness and animosity of a broken family," he says. "I saw siblings with a ton of potential have their opportunities short-circuited because of their bad decisions. I have a brother, Chuck, who was an outstanding basketball player but got kicked out of school four times and the last time for good."

"When my brother Raymond was 18," Fitzhugh continues, "he was one of the best running backs in the state of Ohio and was offered full scholarships by colleges all across the country. But he fell victim to crack abuse and died at the age of 41."

Amid all the darkness, a ray of sunshine finally broke through and gave Fitzhugh the chance to make a decision of his own. When he was 12, his sister started attending church with a boyfriend who eventually left for a Bible college. Wanting some company, she asked her little brother to tag along. That was in January 1975.

Six months later, sometime in June, Fitzhugh was riding home from church with his sister, and she asked him if he had ever accepted Jesus in his heart.

"And I said, 'No, I haven't,'" he recalls. "So my sister prayed the prayer of faith with me as we sat there in the driveway. And the rest is history. That was the first time I found out there was a plan. It just changed everything, because somewhere deep in my mind, I knew that life as I was experiencing it wasn't the way it was supposed to be. When I found out God had a plan for my life, it was an 'ah-ha' moment for me. I jumped onto it and held on to it, and it revolutionized my life."

Fitzhugh now had the strength to say no to drugs and alcohol. He was able to avoid trouble at school and steer clear of the distractions that had beset his parents and siblings. And even when Fitzhugh's sister fell away from God and stopped attending church, he was determined to stay the course.

"I rode the church van every Sunday by myself until I graduated from high school," he says. "I can count how many times I missed on one hand. I wanted to be what I was supposed to be doing. Part of it was discipline, and part of it was the fact that I didn't want to end up where the rest of my family was. They didn't have the plan. I had the plan. I wanted to know more about the plan. I wanted a healthy relationship with Jesus Christ. I wanted everything God had for me, and I knew that whatever was going to happen was in His hands."

Fitzhugh's commitment to fellowship with other believers and his hunger to know God sustained him throughout his high-school career and carried over to his college days, where he met regularly with various ministry groups on the campus of Miami University of Ohio. He avoided the trappings that so many young athletes fall into and remained faithful to righteous living.

"I can't tell you that I was an alcoholic, and I can't tell you that I was strung out on drugs," Fitzhugh says. "But because of the commitment I made to Christ, the Word of God became a boundary for me. Instead of pulling me out of drama, it kept me from being caught up in drama. It kept me from using steroids. It kept me from getting drunk every weekend. It kept me from becoming a sex maniac. It kept me from manipulating women. The Word of God set boundaries of character for me, and that's how I was able to navigate through high school and college and even the NFL."

Fitzhugh says his relationship with Jesus also made him a better teammate. He now understood that biblical teamwork required Christ-centered confidence and humility. And although he learned the value of teamwork growing up as a three-sport athlete, it was his experience at Miami University of Ohio that turned that knowledge into wisdom.

"I played outside linebacker, and in college the competition was much stiffer and the goals were much loftier," Fitzhugh says. "I had to make sure that no matter what, the quarterback or the toss sweep didn't get outside of me. I had to trust the defensive tackle that if I came up to contain, then he was going to be able to do his part. That's when I realized just how valuable it is to do your part—and do your part well—for the success of the team."

Fitzhugh was learning invaluable lessons about spiritual teamwork as well. The temptations in college were much greater than anything he had faced in high school, and it took a band of Christian brothers—he and his four dedicated suitemates—to brave the battlefield together.

"We needed each other to encourage and build each other up, so we could be what God had called us to be," Fitzhugh says. "We would do that in different ways. Some days we would have a Scripture for the week and if we ran into one of our suitemates, we had to be able to recite that Scripture. It was built-in accountability. We were holding one another up. We knew each other's struggles, and it was important for us to help each other get through this thing as strongly as we could."

After his college career, Fitzhugh spent two years in the NFL, playing with the Denver Broncos. While there, he was nicknamed "Priest."

"I was a man of God and I wasn't ashamed about it," he says. "That was just how I rolled."

Upon retirement from professional sports, he turned his attention toward ministry and got involved with Fellowship of Christian Athletes in the Washington, DC, area, where he currently resides with his wife, Dr. Karen Broussard-Fitzhugh, and daughters Nicole and Siona. Fitzhugh's relationship with FCA grew into a partnership, and today he serves as the national spokesman for One Way 2 Play—Drug Free, which spreads a drug-free message to high schools, colleges and juvenile detention centers across America.

Fitzhugh is also the founder and executive director of PowerMoves, a national youth organization that uses athletics, academics and the arts to inspire young people to succeed.

When he speaks to teenagers and young adults, one of the key points he focuses on is the importance of friends and surrounding yourself with people of character who will become your teammates for life.

"I don't know if it's because I'm getting older or if I have less tolerance," Fitzhugh says, "but there is so much drama in the world, and most of that drama comes about when you're hanging around folks you don't need to be hanging around."

Not only does this apply to friendships, but it also applies when it comes to choosing a spouse—the person with whom you will spend the rest of your life. It's a principle that Fitzhugh can back up with personal experience.

"When I was searching for a wife, I had a little test question I would ask anyone I was dating, just to see where her head was," he reveals. "I would just casually, nonchalantly ask, 'What's your ultimate goal in life?' That seems like an innocent question.

"I had young ladies say they wanted to get their law degree or they wanted to be a doctor, but that wasn't what I wanted to hear," Fitzhugh continues. "When I asked that question to the lady I married, she paused and said, 'My ultimate goal in life is to live a life that will be pleasing to my heavenly Father.' Now, I can marry somebody like that. And the reality is, that's how I choose who I'm going to hang out with. There are some people who use certain kinds of language and have certain behaviors and attitudes that I choose not to enjoy downtime with. I don't want to be in situations where they're going to push me in directions I don't want to go."

The Bible is full of similar advice. Proverbs 22:24-25 tells us, "Don't make friends with an angry man, and don't be a companion of a hot-tempered man, or you will learn his ways and entangle yourself in a snare." The apostle Paul takes it a step further when he says in 2 Corinthians 6:14, "Do not be mismatched with unbelievers." And in verse 17, he reminds us of God's admonishment to "come out from among them and be separate."

Choosing godly friends isn't about taking the fun out of life, as so many young believers are often fooled into believing. Rather, God's desire is to protect us from the dangers that come from spending too much time with people who are going in the opposite direction of righteousness and have no interest in seeking after His will for their lives. The negative effect of disobeying this principle is something Fitzhugh has seen time and time again in the lives of young people and adults alike.

"If I can hang out with your good friends for a few minutes, I will then be able to come back to you and predict all of the things in life you'll accomplish or all of the things in life you should stop dreaming about because it isn't going to happen as long as you're rolling with them," Fitzhugh says. "We are very impressionable beings. It's so important who we decide to spend time with. The wrong company can corrupt good morals."

There's an old Japanese proverb that says, "When the character of a man is not clear to you, look to his friends." This also rings true with Fitzhugh, who often uses professional athletes as examples of what happens when poorly selected friends end up derailing a train loaded with potential and promise.

"There are so many great athletes who have made horrible decisions," he says. "I wonder how many of them made horrible decisions because they were someplace they shouldn't have been with people they shouldn't have

141

been hanging with. Very rarely does somebody just get up and say, 'I'm going to go rape, pillage and plunder.' There's always somebody saying, 'Come on. Let's go over here and have some fun.'

"People don't plan on crazy stuff happening," he adds. "But crazy stuff happens, and too often it's because we're linked up with people who are going in a different direction. You've got to be able to say, 'Let's go this way' or you've got to cut them off and let them go."

Fitzhugh equates the two types of friends with eagles and chickens. The eagles are those friends who will support one another and build each other up. The chickens are those friends who lack moral integrity and the discipline to consistently make godly decisions. While eagles soar, the chickens stay on the ground, because, quite simply, they don't know how to fly.

"There are too many eagles who don't have the courage to cut off those one or two chickens who are hanging around," Fitzhugh says. "I've experienced that so often with young people and adults who 'woulda, coulda, shoulda,' but there was a chicken in the midst. That's what happened to my brother. My brother had a chicken in his life who kept giving him malt liquor, and he didn't know that malt liquor would take the next 25 years of his life. He was an eagle who never got off the ground."

Many times it's not the obvious temptations—such as drugs, alcohol or promiscuous sexual behavior—that keep people from reaching their goals in life. Fitzhugh believes that how you live your life usually boils down to simply making a choice between the smooth, wide road that leads to mediocrity or the rocky, narrow road that leads to excellence.

"It's so attractive sometimes to hang out with the chickens because there's not much required of you," explains Fitzhugh. "You don't have to push yourself. You can stay in the chicken coop and eat chicken feed and stay away from the three-foot chicken fence, but you'll never soar and touch the sky. You'll never experience those things. There are a lot of eagles who never soar like an eagle because they spend so much time where it's comfortable with the chickens."

Fitzhugh finds personal inspiration to resist the easy way out in Deuteronomy 23:14: "For the LORD your God walks throughout your camp to protect you and deliver your enemies to you; so your encampments must be holy. He must not see anything improper among you or He will turn away from you."

"God is in my camp, or you can even say, 'God is in my training camp,' to protect me," Fitzhugh expounds. "In other words, He's watching my back. And He's there to deliver my enemies to me. So if He's going to send my enemies to me, I've got to bind them up and send them away. Your camp must be holy. You have to make sure there's nothing wicked in your life, or He'll see it and turn from you. But the Lord is in my camp. This is God's thing. He is up in my camp to protect me and to deliver me. He's on my team, and I have to make sure I'm representing Him on His team."

In the book of Acts, we find an awe-inspiring team of believers who show us what holy encampments look like and what can happen when a group of individuals decide to soar like eagles and remove the chickens from their midst. It was the Day of Pentecost, and the apostle Peter had just preached a message that resulted in 3,000 conversions to the Christian faith.

Then, in Acts 4:42, we read that the followers of Christ "devoted themselves to the apostles' teaching, to fellowship, to the breaking of bread, and to prayers." After that, many miracles took place and signs and wonders began to follow them; and in verse 47 we learn that "every day the Lord added to them those who were being saved." In this ultimate example of teamwork, the early Christians worked together as a unified body. They did so by separating themselves from anyone who might desire to pull them apart. They did so by choosing to soar with eagles.

Fitzhugh says the same thing must happen today if we ever want to see positive changes in our personal lives, in our families, in our churches and in our neighborhoods. We can't be afraid of losing some friends along the way if we ever want to fully realize the destiny that God has planned for our lives.

"It's a short-term sacrifice for a long-term gain," says Fitzhugh. "I'm willing to experience the brief disappointment I'm going to have because you're mad at me because

I wouldn't go with you so that in life I can reach the heights I've been designed to reach. We all have the capacity to soar like eagles."

TRAINING TIME

1. What are the important qualities you look for when choosing your friends? Can you think of a time when having the right friends pushed you to excel or helped you through a tough time?

2. In college, Steve Fitzhugh learned the value of good friends and teammates both on and off the field. Who are some of your closest friends? How have your friendships played into your spiritual life?

3. Read Proverbs 22:24-25. Besides a hot temper, what are some attitudes or characteristics that you should try to avoid when choosing friends?

4. Read 2 Corinthians 6:14-18. Why do you think the apostle Paul takes such a harsh stance against having unsaved friends? Can you describe a situation where you had to separate yourself from a friend in order to move forward in your faith? How difficult was that decision? What was the end result?

5. Read Deuteronomy 23:14. What do you think a holy camp should look like? Read Acts 2:41-47. What are some things that this group of like-minded friends accomplished? What are some goals that you and your Christian friends have achieved? What are some dreams that you hope to accomplish as you choose to soar with eagles?

"The best advice I ever received was from Oscar Roan, a retired tight end with the Cleveland Browns. It was the summer before my first year in college, and he was giving his testimony at my church. After his presentation, I stuck my chest out, threw my shoulders back and carried my 173 pounds up to the front to ask a question. I said, 'Mr. Roan, I've got a full scholarship to Miami University of Ohio. Can you give me some advice? I'd like to play in the NFL one day.' And what he told me shaped my college career. He said, 'Son, the first thing you do when you get to college is find the people who know how to pray, and build relationships with them.' I wasn't ready for that. That was his advice, and I took it. When I got to college, I hooked up with other Christian athletes on campus. I built relationships with those guys, and they were my teammates. They were the guys who I met with once a week. Later I found that some of the African-American players on the team weren't plugged into a Bible study. So at that time, I felt led to start one for them. It grew to be very strong, and it was those guys who hung out together on Saturday nights. When everyone else was out partying and doing all kinds of crazy stuff, we'd get a six-pack of cream soda and go home and watch TBN."

—Steve Fitzhugh

12

FIRM FOUNDATIONS

John Wooden
Former UCLA Head Men's Basketball Coach

How good and pleasant it is when brothers can live together!
It is like fine oil on the head, running down on the beard,
running down Aaron's beard, on his robes. It is like the dew of
Hermon falling on the mountains of Zion. For there the LORD
has appointed the blessing—life forevermore.
PSALM 133:1-3

Coming together is a beginning. Keeping together is progress.
Working together is success.
HENRY FORD

If you hear someone extolling the virtues of teamwork, it's usually within the context of a group of people pressing toward a common goal or successful result. That's certainly something you would expect to hear from legendary UCLA head coach John Wooden, who led the Bruins to an unprecedented 10 NCAA men's basketball championships between 1963 and 1975. But in an age when players and coaches are primarily judged by wins and losses or by individual performance, too often the journey from point A to point B is overlooked, even though there can be significant contentment found in the process alone.

Wooden, who has never been as concerned with winning as most would assume, is reminded of a time when he was working with his book publisher on some marketing items. Two representatives from the company, Amber Ong and Steve Lawson, had brought him 30 basketballs to sign. Ong would hand him a basketball, and Lawson would read the name of the person to whom each autographed item would be sent.

At one point during the assembly line, Wooden paused for a moment and said to Lawson, "This is teamwork." It was an authentic reflection of the true joy that working together with others has always fostered.

"Sometimes we fail to realize how important others are to us," Wooden says. "I think that teamwork really starts out in the home. Children have to help in various ways, and that must be taught when they're young. I think parenting is the most important profession in the world. If children are taught to be considerate of others and think of others and help others in every way they can, they're going to have a much better life, and they're going to be content with themselves."

Wooden's sentiment is eloquently portrayed by David in Psalm 133. Verse 1 says, "How good and pleasant it is when brothers can live together!" This psalm, which can be extrapolated to the teamwork model, ends in verse 3 with the promise that within this model of harmony "the LORD has appointed the blessing—life forevermore."

Contentment is one of the underpublicized benefits of teamwork. But just like anything of value, a solid foundation must first be laid. For Wooden, there are a handful of principles that absolutely must come into play for effective teamwork to be achieved. First on the list is friendship, which sadly is not as prominent within the college and, especially, professional ranks these days. Yet according to Wooden, the best teams have this foundation at their core.

"Friendship is doing for others while they are doing for you," he says. "It's called ministry when all of the doing goes in one direction. Friendship goes both ways. Friendship is like a good marriage—it's based on mutual concern. Friends help each other; they don't use each other. If we are going to successfully work with others, it is vital to know the role of friendship. Friendship comes from mutual esteem and devotion."

Friendship breeds the next key element of teamwork—loyalty. Wooden describes loyalty as a "foundational quality that gets us through hard times." It speaks to our integrity and must be in place for any team to succeed. "In basketball, we want to know if we can count on our teammates," Wooden says. "When we know that they will be there to support us in tight spots, we are more likely to go the extra mile when they too need help. That combination makes each of us better. Loyalty is the force that forges individuals into a team. It's the component that moves teams toward great achievements. That's why, as a coach, I always stressed it."

While loyalty is an emotional characteristic of team-work, reliability puts that dependable attitude into ac-tion. It's more than just a promise to stick by someone's side. It's the proving ground by which others know they can depend on us.

"They know that we will make the effort to do our best, whatever the situation might be," Wooden explains. "They know we won't run, cower or become paralyzed by fear. They have learned to count on our consistency and trustworthiness. We'll still be there making the effort to do our best long after the weaker ones have faded. People can bet the farm on us and still be able to sleep at night. Reliability earns the respect of those around us."

But while many might stop there, Wooden digs even deeper and peels back another layer to reveal the impor-tant component identified as "consideration." The Early Church—as portrayed in the book of Acts—grew consid-erably thanks to this dying principle.

For instance, in Romans 12:10, we are told to "show family affection to one another with brotherly love. Outdo one another in showing honor." This concept is further promoted in Hebrews 10:24, a passage that reminds us to "be concerned about one another in order to promote love and good works."

151

"In a way, I think that plain courtesy is teamwork to me," Wooden says. "When our team went on trips, I was insistent with my players that they treat waiters, hostesses and janitors just as if they were the presidents of a university. I think consideration for others can make someone a better team player, and I think it makes them better at everything."

When all of these foundational elements conjoin, a strong bond is formed, and an irrepressible team spirit is forged. Wooden refers to this as "the ultimate expression of interdependence." It also embodies the kind of unity described in 1 Corinthians 12:26: "So if one member suffers, all the members suffer with it; if one member is honored, all the members rejoice with it."

"Just as team spirit embraces an element of enthusiasm, it also houses a component of cooperation," he says. "But where cooperation makes others better, team spirit makes the group better. Team spirit is consideration, respect and dignity for others. I believe that if heads of state throughout this troubled world of ours truly had more consideration for others, our problems would not be as severe. I'm not saying we wouldn't be without problems. Trouble will always exist. But if we display true consideration for others, most of our problems will be manageable."

When teaching these principles, Wooden often relied on the time-honored coaching tradition of correction—even if it meant keeping a star player out of the game. He strongly believed—and still believes—in the wisdom found in Proverbs 3:11-12: "Do not despise the LORD's instruction, my son, and do not loathe His discipline; for the LORD disciplines the one He loves, just as a father, the son he delights in."

"I found the bench to be the greatest ally I had to make individuals comply with what was best for the team," Wooden says. "As a result, we lost a few games but developed character in the lives of many young men. We won more championships than any other team ever has, but more important, we developed champions on and off the court."

And that brings us back to contentment, that oft-forgotten benefit of teamwork. While so many people struggle to find meaning in worldly measures of success, Wooden knows how a godly view can last a lifetime and then some.

"I don't believe there's any greater joy than finding out that something you have said or done has been meaningful to another, particularly when it was done without any thought of something in return," Wooden says. "If I'm remembered as someone who was considerate of all others, that would make me very happy."

TRAINING TIME

1. What are some seemingly nondescript ways that team-work has found its way into your life? How did work-ing with others on simple tasks make you feel after the fact?

2. Coach Wooden says that we sometimes "fail to real-ize how important others are to us." Who are some important people in your life who you sometimes take for granted? What are some ways that you can show appreciation for them?

3. What is your definition of loyalty? Why do you think loyalty is so important to teamwork? What are some examples of loyalty that you have experienced? What about disloyalty? What differing effects did those two actions have on the team dynamic?

4. Read Romans 12:10. How do you think consideration can improve a team's chemistry? In what ways would a lack of consideration do harm to a team's chem-istry? What are some ways that you show considera-tion to others on your team or in your group?

5. Read 1 Corinthians 12:26. What are some ways you can celebrate the success of a teammate or friend? What are some ways that you can comfort them in times of sorrow and grief?

"Cooperation is working with others for the benefit of all. It is not sacrificing for someone else's benefit. If what you are doing doesn't help everyone involved, then it is something other than cooperation—perhaps you would call it ministry, service or selfishness. My first national championship team (1964) probably operated as a team as much as any team I have ever seen. I'll never forget the conversation between coaches before our final game against Duke. The Blue Devils had two players who stood six foot ten. We didn't have anyone over six foot five. The general consensus was that UCLA was a fine little team, but Duke was a fine big team. However, a European coach observed, 'UCLA will win because they are a team.' I considered that a nice compliment. Running our press was the ultimate test of the cooperative spirit. Every player had to cover for somebody else, and they had to trust each other to do that. When applying our press, the team came to expect to make at least two runs each game during which we would score six to eight points in a row. I believe the players collectively looked for whoever was able to help the team most on any given night, rather than always looking to one individual. The abilities of the players served the team, as opposed to the players being used to serve an individual. That's cooperation."

—John Wooden

THANKS

Fellowship of Christian Athletes would like to give honor and glory to our Lord and Savior Jesus Christ for the opportunities we have been given to impact so many lives and for everyone who has come alongside us in this ministry.

The four core values are at the heart of what we do and teach. Many people have helped make this series of books on these values a reality. We extend a huge thanks to Chad Bonham for his many hours of hard work in interviewing, writing, compiling and editing. These books would not have been possible without him. Thanks also to Chad's wife, Amy, and his two young sons, Lance and Cole.

We also want to thank the following people and groups for their vital contributions: Les Steckel, Tony Dungy, Jackie Cook, the Indianapolis Colts, Shaun Alexander, Todd Gowin, John Wooden, Cat Whitehill, U.S. Soccer Federation, Andy Pettitte, Randy Hendricks, Luke Ridnour, Curtis Brown, Scott Emmert, the San Jose Sharks, Sam Hornish Jr., Melanie Hamilton, Penske Racing, Tamika Catchings, Tauja Catchings, Kevin Messenger, the Indiana Fever, Steve Fitzhugh, Mark Knowles, Matt Fitzgerald, Chris Kaiser, Drew Dyck, *New Man* Magazine and Dave Bartlett.

Thanks to the entire FCA staff, who every day faithfully serve coaches and athletes. Thanks to our CEO and president, Les Steckel, for believing in this project. Thanks to the home office staff: Bethany Hermes, Tom Rogeberg, Dan Britton, Jill Ewert, Shea Vailes and Ken Williams. Thanks also to Bill Greig III, Bill Schultz, Steven Lawson, Mark Weising, Aly Hawkins, and everyone at Regal Books.

IMPACTING THE WORLD FOR CHRIST THROUGH SPORTS

Since 1954, the Fellowship of Christian Athletes has challenged athletes and coaches to impact the world for Jesus Christ. FCA is cultivating Christian principles in local communities nationwide by encouraging, equipping, and empowering others to serve as examples and make a difference. Reaching more than 2 million people annually on the professional, college, high school, junior high and youth levels, FCA has grown into the largest sports ministry in the world. Through FCA's Four Cs of Ministry—coaches, campus, camps, and community—and the shared passion for athletics and faith, lives are changed for current and future generations.

Fellowship of Christian Athletes
8701 Leeds Road • Kansas City, MO 64129
www. fca.org • fca@fca.org • 1-800-289-0909

COMPETITORS FOR CHRIST

FELLOWSHIP OF CHRISTIAN ATHLETES COMPETITOR'S CREED

I am a Christian first and last.
I am created in the likeness of God Almighty to bring Him glory.
I am a member of Team Jesus Christ.
I wear the colors of the cross.

I am a Competitor now and forever.
I am made to strive, to strain, to stretch and to succeed in the arena of competition.
I am a Christian Competitor and as such, I face my challenger with the face of Christ.

I do not trust in myself.
I do not boast in my abilities or believe in my own strength.
I rely solely on the power of God.
I compete for the pleasure of my Heavenly Father, the honor
of Christ and the reputation of the Holy Spirit.

My attitude on and off the field is above reproach—my conduct beyond criticism.
Whether I am preparing, practicing or playing,
I submit to God's authority and those He has put over me.
I respect my coaches, officials, teammates, and competitors out of respect for the Lord.

My body is the temple of Jesus Christ.
I protect it from within and without.
Nothing enters my body that does not honor the Living God.
My sweat is an offering to my Master. My soreness is a sacrifice to my Savior.

I give my all—all the time.
I do not give up. I do not give in. I do not give out.
I am the Lord's warrior—a competitor by conviction and a disciple of determination.
I am confident beyond reason because my confidence lies in Christ.
The results of my effort must result in His glory.

Let the competition begin.
Let the glory be God's.

Sign the Creed • Go to www.fca.org

FELLOWSHIP OF CHRISTIAN ATHLETES COACH'S MANDATE

Pray as though nothing of eternal value is going
to happen in my athletes' lives unless God does it.

Prepare each practice and game as giving "my utmost for His highest."

Seek not to be served by my athletes for personal gain, but seek
to serve them as Christ served the church.

Be satisfied not with producing a good record, but with producing good athletes.

Attend carefully to my private and public walk with God, knowing that the
athlete will never rise to a standard higher than that being lived by the coach.

Exalt Christ in my coaching, trusting the Lord will then draw athletes to Himself.

Desire to have a growing hunger for God's Word, for personal
obedience, for fruit of the spirit and for saltiness in competition.

Depend solely upon God for transformation—one athlete at a time.

Preach Christ's word in a Christ-like demeanor, on and off the field of competition.

Recognize that it is impossible to bring glory to both myself
and Christ at the same time.

Allow my coaching to exude the fruit of the Spirit,
thus producing Christ-like athletes.

Trust God to produce in my athletes His chosen purposes,
regardless of whether the wins are readily visible.

Coach with humble gratitude, as one privileged to be God's coach.

FELLOWSHIP OF
CHRISTIAN ATHLETES

Copyright Fellowship of Christian Athletes, 2003. Revised from "The Preacher's Mandate."